M000296730

FREE FROM SILENCE

12 Success Stories of Overcoming Secrets, Sadness, and Shame

By Visionary Author: Ayanna Mills Gallow

Co-Authors: Amika Reynolds, MD, Brian E. Lewis, Chanel Rose Budd, Cylia Williams-Staton, D. Arlando Fortune, Dr. Adrienne Michelle Horn, Dr. Janell Jones, Kisha L. Clarke, Larsche Reaves, Sharita Davis, and Pastor Cassandra Brown

---

DISCLAIMER

Any information, characters, and events within the compilation of stories or other related and linked materials are the sole opinion of each individual author and are for entertainment use only. The views expressed have no relation to those of any academic, hospital, office practice, or corporate institutions with which the authors are affiliated. Neither the author or co-authors are dispensing medical or legal advice and do not intend any of this information to be used for self-diagnosis, treatment, or legal strategy. Never disregard professional medical or legal advice or delay in seeking it because of something you have read in this book or in any related and linked materials. If you think you may have a medical emergency, call your doctor or emergency room immediately. To the maximum extent permitted by law, the author, related entities, and the publisher disclaim all responsibility and liability to any person, arising directly or indirectly from any person taking or not taking action based on the information provided.

Copyright © 2020 Ayanna Gallow

Thanx A Mills, LLC

Alpharetta, GA, USA

All rights reserved

https://thanxamills.com/

No part of this book may be reproduced, or stored in a retrieval system, or transmitted in any form or by any means, electronic, mechanical, photocopying, recording, or otherwise, without express written permission of the publisher.

ISBN: 978-1-7347709-6-4

Library of Congress Control Number: 2020911668

All scriptures were taken from The King James Bible unless otherwise specified.

TABLE OF CONTENTS

ACKNOWLEDGMENTS

I give honor to God from whom all my blessings flow. To each author who broke their silence to contribute to such an ambitious and worthy project: I am in awe of your strength, faith, and humility. Your stories are powerful beyond measure, and I have no doubt that they will help a multitude of people find the courage to speak up, fight, and overcome obstacles in their lives.

To Kevin T. Robertson (KTR): My eternal gratitude for your far-reaching vision, inspirational leadership, and endless encouragement.

To our editor, Dr. Adrienne Michelle Horn: Thank you for helping us bring clarity and polishing our testimonies so that we may share them with the world.

Finally, a heartfelt thanks to our special loved ones, near and far, who are our biggest cheerleaders and tireless supporters in all of our endeavors. Your encouragement has meant the world to us as we have broken "Free From Silence."

FOREWORD

Kevin T. Robertson

In the shadows of brokenness exist earth-shattering, breath-taking secrets of devastation and pain that millions of people live with each day.

Silence is the voice that can translate peaceful meditation. However, there are over 16,000 acts of horrific violence and abuse each of us witnessed by the age of 16, altering our ability to manage a healthy, emotional IQ.

With that being said, the question is: How does one find a rest haven for silence in a world full of chaotic distractions that will break the sound barrier and violate peace?

The answer is found in these 12 stories of sharing secrets, living in silence, and overcoming shame. This book is the gateway to learn how to speak the truth and break free from the bondage of self-desecration.

Without freedom, it is impossible to live without limitations or create opportunities that will elevate you above the guilt, anger, pain, suffrage, and the systemic effects of other people projecting their abuse on you.

This book is a new opportunity for you to gain clairvoyance and take control of overpopulated thought patterns of darkness that stop you dead in your tracks from leading a productive existence. These 12 courageous authors will absolutely illuminate your path, inspiring your self-fulfilling purpose and lead you to new horizons beyond your current capabilities.

These 12 stories will provide comfort where you have struggled for years, help you pull your head out of the lost sands of time, serve as a launching pad for a new way of thinking, equip you with the education of self-worth and connect you with source energy sparking the confidence of unbreakable molds of stability.

How long are you going to stay silent and let your abusers and oppressors control your every move? How long are you going to let abusive situations control your destiny? How long are you going to keep these deep-seated secrets under wraps with no action plan in place for healing?

How long are you going to reside in the muck and mire of obscurity and sadness? How long are you going to wallow in self-pity and shame yourself so low that you remain at a point of no return? What is your desire for a better quality of life to enact positive change for the better?

Free from Silence: 12 Success Stories of Overcoming Secrets, Sadness, and Shame is a blueprint to break your silence, develop an attitude of boldness and possess the strength to reach the pinnacle of newfound joy NOW!

It's time to put an end to the personal setbacks, business losses, family drama, evaporating friends, disloyal associates, debilitating heartbreak, and broken promises and take control of your life like never before with an authoritative stance of self-discipline and emotional control.

Welcome to your place of peace and the stress-free zone of healing that you've finally been waiting for. It's time to activate your passions and accelerate the full manifestation of your dreams.

-KTR

INTRODUCTION

Ayanna Mills Gallow

Do you believe that a dyslexic child could grow up and become a doctor? What about someone who grew up in dysfunction and later married into chaos? Could he or she become a relationship therapist or Life Coach?

Those scenarios are hard to fathom because it involves people who have experienced trauma. Although studies show that the majority of people will experience trauma by the age of 18, it's still hard to believe that people can be triumphant over their tragedies. Why is that? Perhaps it's because we live in the age of InstaPhotos, where you can go from a blemished face to flawless in minutes or because you can have weight loss surgery and lose 100 pounds in 3 months.

Those are examples of what takes place in society. Therefore, when an ordinary person experiences challenges, they become withdrawn due to the guilt and shame of not magically erasing their problems. This can cause extreme secrets and sadness due to concealment and denial of the truth. It saddens me when someone takes their own life, leaving family members perplexed about what went wrong in their seemingly perfect life. This is disheartening, to say the least.

I know oh too well what it is like to experience secrets, sadness, and shame. However, I overcame my silence, which resulted from my childhood trauma, and now I speak out and coach others to speak out and overcome theirs. Allow me to introduce myself, the origin and name of this book, my transformation, and my purpose in *Free From Silence: 12 Success Stories of Overcoming Secrets, Sadness, and Shame.*

My Silence

My name is Ayanna Mills Gallow, MBA, 10x+ bestselling author, Evangelist, Professional Speaker, Real Estate Investor, Literary Strategist, and my favorite, "mom." Sounds pretty good, doesn't it? It's because that's what I wanted you to know. I used to be embarrassed about certain parts of my life, but the more I speak about those things, the freer I feel. I broke my silence, which in turn helped me to break free of my shame.

No More Silence

Let me add to who I am without omitting the imperfections. I am amongst the 1% of people conceived in rape. My father raped my mother when she was 12 years old, and I was born six weeks after my mother's 13th birthday.

If you think that sounds bad, then let me add to that by saying the rapist was my mother's stepfather, and I grew up in the house with both of them. Traumatic, I know. That experience caused me to be silent because silence was the go-to method in my family. Although I knew the truth of my birth since I was 5, my mother and I did not discuss it until I was 17 after my biological father died.

Secrets, Sadness & Shame

Whenever someone would say, "I heard your grandfather was your father," I denied it as if it couldn't be true. Technically, I didn't lie about it because he was my step-grandfather. However, I still kept it a secret because everyone else had what I considered to be "a regular dad."

Secret

I kept the secret from my friends, and I even hid what I knew from my mother. I never admitted it until the day someone said, "I heard what your grandfather did to your mom, and it's wrong for people to whisper about it because it's not your fault." Although I wanted to deny it, it helped me to hear another person's point of view. Therefore, not keeping it a secret this particular time added to my healing and my breakthrough.

Sadness

My sadness came because I felt unwanted and unloved. My family took my mother to have an abortion when they found out she was pregnant. However, it was too late in my mother's pregnancy. Knowing this made me feel like my life was a mistake.

Do you know how it feels knowing that your family intended to kill you? Sounds pretty bad, doesn't it? This made me feel unwanted and unloved. I felt as if my life was a mistake. However, I had a big aha moment when I learned that it was actually God who made me and that I wasn't a mistake. The scripture that changed it for me was:

"And the Lord God formed man of the dust of the ground and breathed into his nostrils the breath of life; and man became a living soul."

Genesis 2:7

Shame

My shame came from knowing that the blood that runs through my body came from a rapist. I was so embarrassed that a grown man, my father, would rape a pre-teen girl, my mother. However, I had a mindset shift. I stopped thinking I was the child of a rapist and focused on me being the child of a rape survivor, and more importantly, a child of God.

So how do people overcome secrets, sadness, and shame from childhood trauma? They break their silence so that they can heal.

Free From Silence

In my first novel, *God & Hip Hop: 21 Day Biblical Devotional Inspired By Hip Hop*, I revealed the story of my birth. It shocked many people to learn that I suffered in silence due to the pain of being born to a 13-year-old teenager as a result of rape. It especially surprised those I've known for over 30 years because they had no idea.

Although I tucked my birth story away by putting it on day 13 of 21, it still helped people. I received testimonials from people who were inspired by my story. They were inspired by my life because I was able to achieve success after what I went through.

People began confiding in me about their struggles, even though I am not a counselor. The only regret I had with revealing my truth in God & Hip Hop is that I wished I had stated it more boldly so that I could have impacted more people. That's when I knew I had to do more. I thought, *if one story can have that kind of impact, then how many people can a book of multiple transformational stories impact?* This made me lead a book anthology called *From Glass to Stone: 10 Transformational Stories of Resilience.*

I broke my silence when I tucked away my birth story in God & Hip Hop, but I broke free when I boldly put my story "first" in From Glass to Stone. I am continuing to walk in my truth by putting my transformational story first in this book as well. Nonetheless, the Word of God helped shift my mindset from viewing myself as Unwanted and Unloved to UnWanted and UnLoved.

Overcoming

Transparency helped me to be my true authentic self and go from a silent child to a public speaker. I learned that silence doesn't yield anyone peace. I found my purpose and my voice. The keys to my transformation were growing in my relationship with God through praying and bible reading, surrounding myself with a great support system, listening to Hip Hop music to keep me upbeat, and writing out my thoughts, feelings, and challenges. My motto is "write, pray and release so that you can have peace."

Free From Silence: 12 Success Stories of Overcoming Secrets, Sadness and Shame is comprised of 12 Transformational nonfiction stories that will benefit those who are looking for inspiration and hope after experiencing tough and traumatic times.

The purpose of this book is to share stories of how the co-authors achieved success after being placed in situations that could have inhibited their success. The authors break silence on going through abuse, addiction, death, debt, depression, divorce, dysfunction, dyslexia, incarceration, and sickness. The authors give you a transparent view of the causes and effects of their past problems and how they became successful. Because social media portrays "perfect people" who prosper, the purpose of this book is to break the stigma to show imperfect people who overcame real-life situations.

In conclusion, if you are afraid to ask, "How do I go on," or "How will I make it through the storm," then this book is for you. In this book, the authors reveal their secrets, sadness, and shame, so that you can overcome and be Free From Silence.

A Poem for Your Pain

In the world full of inequalities and violence

We must break our silence

We speak up for what we've overcome

To help you not give up but stand up, fight, and run.

Even when the odds were against us, and we felt outdone

We kept praying and trying until the battle was won.

Some of our battles are still hard and demanding

But we are successful as long as we keep standing

If you don't know how to fix it or what to choose

Taking your own life or hurting others is how you lose.

Don't get lost in a world thinking you don't fit in.

Speak up, seek wise counsel, break free, and WIN

CHAPTER 1

COVERED FROM COVID

Amika Reynolds, MD

Never did I ever imagine, while pursuing medicine, that my career would threaten my life. I have always known since I could think for myself that I wanted to be a physician. My goal was to have an international medical practice to help lives all over the world. However, I never imagined that I would become my own patient and endure the fight of my life. Come with me on this journey of saving lives, fearing for mine, and then fighting to survive.

Becoming

My youngest memories included me drawing pregnant women and fantasizing about what I thought it meant to be a doctor. I imagined that I would be a doctor who delivered babies. It's almost as if that was the only type of doctor that existed. However, as I grew, I learned.

In high school, I chose a topic that placed me in the hospital, and I became a nursing student. I visited patients and learned how to provide basic care. I completed that curriculum and then went on to college. It was there that I implemented the first step to becoming a physician, which was majoring in biology.

After graduation, I applied to medical school and then took the necessary steps to achieve my goal of becoming a physician. Currently, I practice medicine as a hospitalist. Throughout this journey, I realized there was so much more to medicine than delivering babies. Do not get me wrong. I delivered my fair share of babies. However, I found a new niche.

The Pandemic

During the time that I was becoming a physician, I was taught and learned along the way how to protect myself from communicable diseases through various protocols, practices, and habits. It is through these practices that protection becomes a normal way of life. These practices were essential in providing the level of preparedness while dealing with COVID-19 in the hospital. According to the CDC, the Coronavirus disease (COVID-19) is an infectious disease caused by a newly discovered coronavirus. COVID-19 can cause some to experience mild symptoms. However, in the early part of 2020, people in the United States were dying from it. It became a pandemic and a very scary disease.

In the early stages of the pandemic, however, hospitals were not completely prepared. Initially, testing was an issue. Everyone who came in with symptoms was screened intently. ED physicians were looking for code words, such as recent travel or sick contacts. For those who were suspected, testing was still dependent on what was found on imaging either through a chest x-ray or CT scan. But for those who were successfully tested, the results took days to come back. Some of those patients improved and were discharged with no results. The unfortunate ones remained hospitalized and often progressively worsened.

COVID-19

COVID-19 completely changed my life and the way I practiced. In the hospital, I think of when I met my first COVID patient. That night I received a phone call from the emergency department telling me that there was a patient who required admission. According to the report, the patient had recently traveled and come back with fevers and shortness of breath. At that time, the guidelines suggested that recent travel, fever, and shortness of breath were reasons to test for COVID. This patient was tested and was presumed to be positive. I remember the way I felt after the phone call was over. I was scared, to say the least. I did not know how I was going to handle this. After hearing about this virus for months on a different continent and seeing the damage it caused, it was finally here, and I had to face it.

I reviewed the patient's chart while he was in the emergency room. I thought about a plan for his treatment. I thought about how I was going to approach him and what I would do when I was in his room. I remember putting on my mask, my gown, and my gloves. I was in such a panic that my hand started to sweat. I was wearing an N-95 mask, which made it difficult to begin with. I was in such a state of fear that it became even more difficult to breathe.

As I spoke to the patient, I couldn't help but plan my escape. I remember thinking, *can this mask really protect me*? I mean, other healthcare workers were wearing them, according to what I saw, but they were still dying. The first physician in China who brought awareness to the virus had succumbed to the virus. How was I going to protect myself and ultimately save myself? Honestly, at one point, I did not think that I would survive. I knew I shouldn't have thought that way, but I couldn't help it. I thought about changes I needed to make to my life insurance plan that I set up years ago so that my children would be financially secure in my absence. It was a hard thing to think about. It made me cry, but what was the alternative? I took an oath, and I could not give up in this critical time.

The changes that took place with COVID were not just happening at work. I am a single mother of two young girls. My village consists of my immediate family. They have been very important in helping me raise my girls. When COVID finally arrived at my hospital, things changed at home also. My mother decided to take the girls to her home in an effort to keep me isolated, away from them. My mother would take the girls, and she, along with my sister and stepdad, would stay home—no one in, no one out.

At this time, the stay-at-home order was made by Andrew Cuomo, the governor of New York. All nonessential businesses and all schools were to close. Social distancing was put into effect. People were not allowed to gather in large numbers. People were encouraged to stay a minimum of 6 feet away from each other when in public. In the early stages of the pandemic, the CDC did not advise the public to wear masks, thinking that it would create more contamination if used inappropriately. Also, the CDC believed it would create more of a shortage of masks needed by healthcare providers. However, I never agreed with that.

My Contribution

In an effort to combat the problem, I decided to make masks at home. I had never used a sewing machine before, but I believe that desperate times call for desperate measures. One morning, I picked up the phone and called my grand aunt, who was the sewer in our family. I told her what my intentions were and asked if she was on board with making masks for the healthcare workers at my hospital. Without hesitation, she agreed and thus began my homemade masks.

I remember the first time I decided to wear a mask to the supermarket. One wouldn't believe this was such a difficult decision for me, but it was. At this time, the highest cases of infections were in New York City, unlike where I live upstate, so I was one of the few people wearing masks in public. Of course, as I walked into the supermarket, I began getting looks. A gentleman enthusiastically approached me, asking where I got that "Michael Jackson" mask from. I shared my source as we laughed it off, primarily because he called it a Michael Jackson mask. That brief interaction broke the ice for me and allowed me to continue my shopping with more confidence. I never went to work or anywhere in public without my mask. Covering my face to protect myself and others was my new normal.

My Fear Became My Reality

After all the good hygiene practices, within the first couple of months of the pandemic in the United States, I tested positive for COVID-19. All of my fears for my life and the livelihood of my family was starring me in the face. However, instead of giving up, I went from fearing the consequence of the COVID-19 to inheriting it and finding ways to conquer it!

One night while I was at work, I started to experience changes in my body. It first started with excessive tiredness. Despite sleeping for the majority of the previous day into that morning, I still felt tired. Throughout the night, I started to experience chills intermittently and noticed that my arms and legs were tender. My back was also hurting constantly. I battled with the thought of possibly being COVID positive. However, denial set in, and it was strong. *How could I possibly be positive? After all, I've been taking the necessary precautions.* I started thinking back about a patient room that I was in that was presumed to have a high viral load secondary to that patient being intubated. I thought about my interactions with patients on other days prior where I may have been exposed or let my guard down. Finally, I thought about the one night that I wore a mask that didn't seem to fit tightly enough. *Could that have been my demise? When could this have happened? How? Did I get too comfortable?*

Approaching the end of my shift, I decided to take Tylenol for the aches that I felt in my back and my extremities. I even took my temperature, and it was normal. However, I just couldn't shake the feeling that something was not right. I went to employee health immediately after my shift was over. My temperature at that time had elevated despite taking Tylenol. This made me more concerned. I was tested via a nasopharyngeal swab and was told to await my results, which would be ready an hour later. I drove home with the possibility that I might be infected. What was I going to do if I was positive? I was hoping my feelings were wrong, primarily because I had advocated for so long. How could I be the one to fall ill? In retrospect, I was beginning to feel shame.

My results came back positive. Of course, I started thinking of the worst scenarios. I was treating dying patients, and I knew that I could be next. The more the news sunk in, the more paranoid and emotional I became. Oh, I cried. That was necessary. But when I was done crying, I started to create a plan.

#1. I prayed to God.

#2. I reached out to my former residency class, which consisted of 10 other medical doctors I graduated with. It was one of the best decisions I made. This group of doctors was able to give me advice, recommendations on drugs and therapy, and updates about COVID-19 at their locations, which are located across the world.

#3. I called my financial advisor to make sure my affairs were in order and to create a will and trust. I picked a health care proxy, a trustee, and an estate planner.

#4. I started self-medicating with homemade remedies. My mother made garlic tea with lime and orange peel. My grandmother made chicken soup from scratch. I was prescribed medication, which at the time was thought to be helpful. My aunt set up video surveillance so that I could be seen while at home alone. I began taking vitamins.

#5. I woke up every morning to exercise. I also monitored my vitals daily. My village began praying for me on social media and via telephone. My spirit was lifted with the outpouring of support that came from social media from my friends, my family, and even people I didn't know.

#6. I gave advice to and prayed for others who tested positive. I shared what I was eating and drinking.

#7. I journaled. I wrote daily about how I was feeling. I wrote detailed information to include my temperature, my emotions, my goals for the day, and more.

COVID didn't stand a chance! After two days of experiencing those symptoms, I reported I became symptom-free. Eleven days later, I tested negative. I am convinced now that this was all God's plan! I contracted the disease I feared the most, but I conquered it and won!

Conclusion

I went from fearing the consequences of COVID-19 to acquiring the infection and finding solutions to combat it, and ultimately, beating it. I feel freer now because there is a large part of me that realizes that I don't have to run anymore. The worst has happened; my greatest fear came true. I only have God to thank for the positive outcome. Not only did God allow me to beat the virus, but He also allowed me to become an author for the first time with the release of my COVID journal. I also started a small business, revived some old relationships, and became closer to GOD during my solidarity. Due to COVID-19, I have a success story; I have a testimony. I went from fear to finding solutions, which resulted in me becoming more successful than I was before. I had COVID-19, but God covered me.

CHAPTER 2

From Unwanted
to Purpose Driven

Brian E. Lewis

As a child, I dealt with trauma, neglect, and mental abuse and harbored feelings well into my adulthood that affected relationships, friendships, and my professional life. For years, I kept my thoughts inside, and over time, those thoughts transformed into emotional chains. Eating away at me from the inside out, the pain held me back from becoming the man I was destined to be. By breaking my silence, I also broke those emotional chains. By telling my story, I hope to give courage to children and adults who've been affected by trauma or neglect. We must take care of our children and the well-being of our society. "Protecting our kids is protecting our future."

Line in the Sand

The National Institute of Mental Health defines childhood trauma as the experience of an event by a child that is emotionally painful or distressful, which often results in lasting mental and physical effects. Nearly 35 million US children have experienced childhood trauma, and more than 33% of our youth have faced traumatic events by the age of 16. Trauma affects not only our youth but adults as well. In the US, 61% of men and 51% of women have been exposed to at least one traumatic event. Regardless of who experiences a traumatic event, it is a problem in our society that needs to be addressed. Childhood trauma bleeds well into adulthood and has been linked to numerous health issues, including diabetes, depression, substance abuse, and suicide attempts.

How Many Words Does This Picture Say?

Unhealthy and unwanted. This was my birth in a nutshell. Born premature, weighing in at 2 lbs and up for adoption. Even though my mom changed her mind about *keeping* me, I'm not sure she changed her mind about *wanting* me.

I wasn't supposed to be part of their family, and this was evident in their "family picture" -- a picture of all siblings except me. I was never later added, nor did we take another one. The hurt I felt as a kid when I got left out was worse than any beating I got.

When I was ten, I witnessed my first death. My buddy and I were playing near his home when we noticed his aunt pull up, park, and go inside the house. Moments later, his two-year-old baby sister began running after a ball that had rolled behind the car. Suddenly the car rolled back over her head, killing her instantly.

As I got older, the nightmares got bad as my home life worsened. Noticeable favor shown to my siblings extinguished my esteem, and the reason was evident. We had different fathers.

First, I blamed and cursed my biological father for not being around, and honestly, he still deserves that blame; he had plenty of chances to reach out to me. When I finally met him at 14, my mother, grandmother, and I pulled up to his home, which happened to only be three blocks from my granny's house. I was always at granny's house. His first words to my mom were, "Why did you tell me he wasn't mine?"

For the first time, I felt cheated out of my father for bearing another man's name. *Why give me the name but not treat me the same?* His statement led me to believe that maybe he would have been there if he knew I was his and bore his name. He never was and actually stood me up twice after that meeting. We never had that "father-son" moment before his death ten years later. It took me two years to cry over his death, realizing I would never know him.

I love my mom and my siblings, but they were programmed to think they were better than me by the favor shown. Once I had to wait three hours after a cold, wet football game because of this favor. Hungry and tired, I sat there watching every teammate drive away with their supportive family. When my mom and brother finally arrived full, dry, and happy, I got the same feeling I get every time I saw "that" picture.

Making the mistake of being mad at my brother, she left me to walk five hours home in my football uniform. I remember walking past several family members' houses who could've given me a ride, but why let them off the hook that easy? I often thought, *if your mom doesn't love you, no one else will.* I got to my lowest point and wanted to kill myself. But I didn't want to die without them knowing that if they had shown me love, I would be alive. I swallowed every pill in the house and went straight to bed, hoping never to wake up, but I did.

Maintenance Required

The trauma, neglect, and abuse I suffered had a stronger hold on me than I was ready to admit to. It left me bashful, bitter, and broken. Honestly, I was a breeding ground for secrets, shame, and sadness. In order to rid yourself of something, you must first understand the meaning of it. What is it?

If one begins repairs on a vehicle, doesn't that person need to know what parts and tools they would use to do the job? Would you solve your car issues with an oil change if all you needed was gas or a new battery? The goal is to save time and money. It's no different with the makeup of the human being. When I began to attack my issues accurately and honestly, life started to become more enjoyable. When I took a closer look into my sadness, which is the condition or quality of being sad, I began to break through to the root causes and, even more importantly, the effects.

The saddest thing I felt was the loss of my brother to prison, and even worse was the welfare of our relationship when he got incarcerated. We had our problems and could barely get along, but he's my brother, and I love him. The amount of time he was sentenced with in comparison to the amount of time he has served is quite enough to forgive him for the most part. I don't feel at fault or responsible for his incarceration, but my presence kept him from doing things that would get him in trouble.

Part of me wonders if he would have gotten locked up if I was around. I would cry heavily in the shower by myself. Not one day went by without me thinking of my brother; it was almost too painful to cope. This led to a downward spiral of events. I wasted years hanging around, smoking weed, partying, and doing all the things I advised my brother not to do. I lost my job, my girlfriend and I started to lose myself. My relationship with my mom began to worsen, and there was constant confusion in my life. I felt extremely guilty because my mom's health began to deteriorate, which later turned into diabetes. I believe my brother being in prison caused excruciating pain for both me and my mom. I wanted to be there for my mom and help her out. However, I couldn't even help myself.

I couldn't keep a job or a date, and I was always alone. In some ways, I felt as if I were the secret, something unknown or not meant to be known or seen by others because nobody cared to see me, which made it easier to convince myself I was not meant to be.

The Tune up

I received a much-needed boost from my granny two weeks before she passed. It was around the time when her memory was starting to fade. Without missing a beat, she saw me and said, "Hey, Brian!" I can't explain how meaningful and heartwarming it was to know she had never forgotten me. Once I began the necessary repairs in the correct target areas on my car (body), it began running better. I started asking, "What can I do to make it better?"

When I found the answers, things started to happen. I discovered my love for the outdoors and the peace of mind obtained when going for walks. I started achieving the goals I would set for myself, got my CDL, and enrolled in the College for Culinary Arts so that I could become a chef. My career has allowed me to travel to some of the most beautiful places across America. My relationship with my mother is at an all-time high. I've gained great friends and colleagues in high places and advanced in my profession with the strength to not only fight for myself but others who don't have the courage to fight for themselves.

Enhanced Model

I went from feeling like a worthless child due to trauma, neglect, and abuse to becoming a confident leader and advocate for forgotten children.

Below are the transformation steps I took to break free to achieve success:

1. **Prayer-** Gaining a relationship with God through Jesus was my greatest accomplishment. With this one action, I could have a best friend, a psychologist, and a father. Growing up in the church provided me with an understanding of the importance of this. I can honestly say, without a doubt, prayer was the catalyst to my success.

2. **Music-** Like most, music provided me with a great way to escape and being eclectic allotted me more options and genres to explore. Music also gives one an insight into other cultures and races, making you feel more connected to others.

3. **Promotions-** Promotions were the "validation" of success. I felt validated every time I received a promotion or raise of pay. Sometimes I would be at my lowest in my personal life, but at my best professionally. Validation provided a great balance in earning a "distraction from distress." I realize my heart and soul believed what the brain heard, even if I didn't.

4. **New Environment-** I've done much soul searching in my time and asked myself what I should do or how I should do it. More times than not, it would come down to change.

5. **Wildlife/Nature-** Most steps I took to better myself stemmed directly from "need" more than "want." Most things you're going to change are going to be needed. One needed thing I did was incorporate nature and outdoors into my life. While outdoors, I felt at peace. I believed that I healed a lot in nature because I was free of judgment from others. I fell in love with nature, and it became an enjoyable hobby and a stress reliever for me.

6. **Relationship Mending-** Repairing and improving my relationship with my mom has filled the biggest hole in my heart. Because of my healing, I was able to give and receive love from her.

Brand New Model

Overcoming the mental stress of neglect and trauma can be extremely difficult for anyone. The stress may never go away. I never forgot the things I experienced. I just gained the strength to overcome them.

Traumatic childhood memories can manifest in nightmares and persist for years. It is my desire to help children to overcome trauma so that they can be successful. This is not a taboo topic. In fact, anyone dealing with the stress of childhood trauma should not allow themselves to be buried by the secrets, shame, or sadness that prevents them from breaking towards the surface for success.

CHAPTER 3

SELF LOVE

Chanel Rose-Budd

Breaking The Cycles of Dysfunctional Relationships

The world remains to be full of deceit, lies, lack of trust, adultery, treason, hate, and all kinds of sinfulness. How do you overcome and live a wholesome life for yourself, children, marriage, and family?

Divorce rates are at an alarming all-time high. According to the statistics via Wikipedia, 50 % of Americans' first marriages end in divorce, followed by 60% of second marriages and 70% of third marriages. Low-income marriages yield on the higher level of results. When we examine these statistics more closely, we will find a disproportionately higher percentage of these numbers reflecting people of color. The numbers are alarming, and there are many reasons why. Yet, the number one reason is lack of knowledge and understanding.

My name is Chanel Rose, and I was born and raised in Pittsburgh, PA. I am the eldest of three children, and I grew up in low-income environments throughout my childhood. My mother and father had an abusive relationship, so she separated from him when I was two years old. I yearned for a father figure, but all the men around me were controlling or abusive and partook in alcohol or a drug substance the majority of the time. Therefore, the only male role model I had was my great grandfather, who had served in the military and lived in a community on the other side of the city.

When I became a teenager, life started to get even more challenging due to peer pressure, gang violence, and drugs flooding the neighborhoods. I had to grow up quickly to defend and protect myself and siblings from those even more broken in our neighborhood. I had dreams and goals as a child that were diminishing. Consequently, I took on the personality of my environment to survive, as did so many others around me.

I started dating with this false sense of self. The first guy I dated broke my virginity and also violated me. I felt shattered, defenseless, and taken advantage of at 15 years old. This experience changed how I viewed relationships with men and my own young body.

I was very well endowed for a young girl. I had to fight off the boys because my breasts were so huge. I remember having to run home because of being chased down by a group of boys in elementary school! What if they would have caught me?

I did not realize it then, but those kinds of traumatic experiences planted a seed in my mind that produced thoughts of distrust toward men. I grew more guarded and more cautious with everyone, not just men. However, the yearning of having a male in my life who loved me was still there.

Love Is Blind

At 17 years old, I met my future husband, whom I call Love. He is the man who would become my child's father not very long after we started dating. My husband had a tough upbringing, similar to mine. His mother was an addict, and his father passed away when he was 19 years old. Our childhoods were very dysfunctional, and I hoped to raise our child better than what we had to endure.

It did not take long to recognize that our dysfunctional upbringings caused us to distrust one another, which led us into years of a game of "tit for tat." Due to several circumstances, we eventually ended our relationship for five years before trying to restore it. At some point, I realized that Pittsburgh did not offer me an environment where I could explore the idea of living my true self.

I eventually moved to Dallas, Texas, and Love joined us a few months later because he wanted a new start as well. We bonded, and it seemed as if my dreams as a child were starting to resurface again. Blinded by the dysfunctional upbringing and behaviors learned throughout our childhood and young adulthood, we had not considered that the bad habits were still apart of us.

I noticed early on that breaking the cycles would be hard work, but I wasn't going to stop trying. Love and I discussed getting married a few years later, and eventually, we tied the knot. The first year of marriage was wonderful. We celebrated with friends from our hometown who had moved to Dallas the year prior.

However, our relationship became more trying due to significant life events, such as Love's son being killed in our hometown at 16 years old by gun violence. After grieving the loss of my stepson, I found out a few years later that Love had been diagnosed with heart failure. The reality of being married and understanding what you think marriage is and what it is not began to sink in on a deeper level for me.

Love was very saddened by the way his life started to unfold while trying to start a better life for himself and his family. We both were in our 30s at this time and having to make major decisions on how to manage the future of our individual goals, health, family, and lifestyle became surreal. I knew this was going to be very challenging for him because socializing and drinking had become his routine.

We communicated about everything, the good and bad, most of the time, but it wasn't easy to get a word in. I began to know my husband more deeply, and if I'm honest, I ignored so many red flags long before we got back together. My husband was always so arrogant and bold with no filter whatsoever. He would make me feel low sometimes from his words. I confronted him with being too friendly to other women since he did not want me to have male friends at all. I just ignored his ways most of the time until he pushed me enough to speak out about how he made me feel.

The biggest issue was his "do as I say and not as I do" mindset. I didn't agree with that, which caused more disagreements and a lack of trust in our relationship. Trusting him was the main issue I had in the past. It was hard for me to express the importance of being able to trust anyone, let alone the man I shared my life with.

I managed to seek counseling and guidance. Also, having a relationship with the Lord kept me grounded no matter the storms. During counseling, I began to have a deeper understanding of myself and the real issues buried deep down inside. I went through generational cycles of trauma. I had been violated as a young teenager, abandoned by my father, forced to help raise my siblings and became a teenage mother.

When the counselor guided me through my past, it became clear that I was damaged and trying to mask it all by moving out of state, getting married, and living as if none of it happened to me. I lacked trust and felt unloved and insecure, which resulted in me having low self-esteem. It had all stemmed from childhood experiences, blossomed in my adulthood, and followed me into my marriage. Although I knew he had experienced traumatic situations and dealt with personal issues of his own, it was time for me to focus on myself.

After counseling sessions ended, I tried to get my husband to attend because it was necessary. We went once as a couple, but at the time, he didn't want to go back. Counseling truly helped me better understand that you have to heal before getting into relationships with another person. Marriage changed me mentally, emotionally, and spiritually. I learned the importance of being healed from the past hurts, equally yoked or at least on one accord before committing to dating, long term relationships, and marriage.

Now I've healed and changed the trajectory of my life, purpose, and marriage, for it was very painful to accept we both were truly broken people trying to find our way through dysfunctional mindsets and behaviors. My husband and I agreed that we each had to be accountable for what happened in our daily lives. I continue to write out my goals, journal, remain aware of my boundaries, pray, and focus on self-care, encouraging myself through words of affirmation and creating a new way of living a better life.

My Transformation

I went from being a woman caught up in the cycles of marital dysfunction to becoming whole and transformed into a relationship and personal development coach.

8 Steps to Transform Yourself and Relationships

Self-Awareness- Process the events and sort out the issues, insecurities, doubts, fear, lack of self-confidence, or any dysfunctional patterns of behaviors of your own. It starts with evaluating yourself first.

Accountability- What can you do to have better control over your actions, shortcomings, or emotions?

Acceptance- Accept your faults and shortcomings. Agree to change for the better. Acknowledge what's happening in your relationship, the good, bad, and indifferent. Accept reality and find ways to grow, heal, and move forward.

Forgiveness- Forgive those who hurt you intentionally or unintentionally because this will allow you to be set free from the mental and emotional bondage the person or issue has caused. Forgive yourself for allowing yourself to hold on to any emotions or feelings, especially those that were in your control. This step is one of the most powerful processes.

Self-Love- Speak life over yourself, telling yourself how beautiful, strong, successful, victorious, and worthy you are. Take at least four days out of each month to pamper yourself with a gift, massage, manicure, pedicure, or movie, just to name a few ideas.

Set Boundaries- Write down what you will and will not tolerate in your space no matter what family, friends, or partners enter your life. Your morals, values, wants, and needs will help you see who you are and what boundaries should never be crossed. The saying is, "People only do what you allow them to do," so this is to assist in breaking the cycle of that mythical truth.

Communication- Communicating to be heard effectively is key, and there are many ways to do so. Speaking to your spouse or loved ones decently and respectfully yields better results. Keep in mind that everyone has a different communication style. It's important to be mindful of your emotions before having conversations from the heart.

Prayer- Praying about your life, current situation, and future is very important as well. Meditating on the Word of the Lord, having faith, and believing in the promises of the Lord helps in all areas of one's life. If you do not pray or have a relationship with the Lord, it's never too late to start. Journal your thoughts, goals, and dreams and then pray about them. You will be surprised how far it will take you.

In conclusion, marriage is a ministry. I feel empowered and refuse to settle for anything less than what my core values are because I know my worth. Dysfunctional cycles can be broken, healing is possible, and relationships are healthier once therapy and self-care begin. My testimony encourages women and men not to allow past traumas to determine the trajectory of your future.

CHAPTER 4

LIFE AFTER DEATH

Cylia Williams-Staton

Healing and Rebuilding after the Loss of My Father

Why is it that everyone experiences grief, but no one is prepared for it? The past three years of my life have completely transformed me. I went from depending solely on my dad to convincing him that I was strong enough for him to rely solely on me for his full-time care and daily needs. I watched my fractured relationship with my mother completely break into pieces so small that you could not see them with the naked eye. I spent many sleepless nights and worried days living and standing on the belief that better days were ahead. GOD would see me through this as HE has kept me through everything else in my life. You could have never convinced me that my life would have such drastic changes and events take place before all of this happened. My dad, who was always the one who supported, uplifted, and helped everyone else, was forever changed when he had to depend on others for his most basic human needs.

Daddy's Girl

My father was my HERO. When he smiled, the sun seemed to beam from his face. He was like magic to me. He could command the attention of anyone, keep you entertained and on the edge of your seat when he spoke, and he always left you feeling like witnessing him in action was something that you would never forget. I loved my daddy, and he loved me in such a way that no one could ever come between us. Everybody would call me a "Daddy's Girl," and I wore it like a badge of honor.

I used to watch Bruce Lee movies with my dad because he loved them, and even though I couldn't read the subtitles yet, I got excitement from watching him get thrilled when Bruce Lee would beat his competition. I would find out later in life's journey that my father was a fighter just like Bruce Lee, but he didn't physically fight people; he fought daily for his family and ultimately for his life when he was diagnosed with an incurable illness at the age of 62.

Faith

I first learned about GOD from my daddy. My daddy loved and trusted GOD with everything in him, and his faith was like none I'd ever seen. Even when he was faced with health issues and his body started to fail him, he never stopped saying that "Every day is getting better." He reminded me so much of Job in the Bible because no matter what happened to him, he always trusted GOD, and he never questioned the path GOD had set for him to take. That is why I was adamant about finding help for my dad when his health started to fail him, and I didn't stop until we had a satisfactory plan of care.

We Need Answers

It started with my dad being diagnosed with and beating prostate cancer. The doctor told us that it could take six months to 2 years before my father regained his full strength and started to feel like himself again. He seemed to be improving around the 1-year mark of his cancer being in remission until he suddenly began to have issues with his balance. He started to trip a lot and wobble and be off-balance when he would stand and walk. His stumbling and falling became worse, and he progressed from a cane to a walker over time.

When the summer months rolled around, he started to get dizzy when he was out and about during the day. At first, we thought it was because he wasn't drinking enough water, but an increase in his water intake didn't fix the problem. We started going to the ER multiple times a week because he would have "spells" that caused him to pass out. They wouldn't last more than a few minutes before he would come back to himself and seem as if nothing happened. The doctors couldn't understand what was happening, and they continued to send us home with different medications for him to "try." It was very frustrating because even though I was happy to hear the doctors say that nothing was wrong with my dad, in my heart, I knew that something wasn't right. We needed to figure it out before things continued to get worse.

In the months to come, my father started to talk with a slur, and the pitch of his voice became extremely high. He would pass out more and more, and I would become more frustrated as the doctors continued to send us home without answers. It was at this time that I started researching my father's symptoms and came across a rare disease called "Multiple Systems Atrophy." I mentioned it to one of the ER doctors on our next visit, but they seemed to brush it off and say they didn't know much about it. I decided to take my father to UNC Chapel Hill to get him looked at by some of the best doctors in our area. It was about a year later when my dad was officially enrolled in their system, and they diagnosed him with the disease that GOD revealed to me over 16 months before. As scared as I was, at least we were finally getting some answers and could come up with a treatment plan.

We went to appointment after appointment, trying many medications, exercises, and plans to find something that worked for my dad. Things were decent for about six months, but then things seemed to take a turn for the worse. My dad was in the hospital multiple times a month, with the stays ranging from three days to two weeks.

It was in September, one month after my first year in my new position as a Kindergarten Teacher, that I received a call from hospice stating that my father would be enrolled in their program because there was nothing else the physicians at the hospital could "medically" do for him. I dropped the phone in shock and cried for the rest of that day. I went to the hospital, and they explained the program and let me know that he had two options: to go home with me or go to a facility. My dad was totally against going to a facility. Although our home was small and crowded, we knew that living with me was the only acceptable option for us.

I went home and rearranged our entire home to get ready for my father to move in. They gave us all the equipment we needed and taught me how to be his in-home CNA. I was terrified, but I knew that GOD would give me the strength I needed to properly care for my dad and comfort him through this process. I called my job and told them the news. Although I was afraid that I would lose my new position, my dad's health was my number one priority, and I would sacrifice the position I loved for my father, whom I loved more than words can express.

I was out of work for months until I was able to get a family member whom we trusted to care for my dad while I worked half days in the classroom. I spent many nights without sleep because I wanted to make sure that everything was okay and that I was meeting the needs of my family, my dad, and myself. My life was forever changed, but it was okay because I was able to spend the last most precious months of my father's life in the same home with him. Although I am grateful for this experience, it led me to some of the greatest grief I have ever experienced in my life.

Grief

Grief is something that everyone will be affected by at some time in their lives. I define grief as a rollercoaster ride of emotions that you did not ask to get on, but you are forced to experience when a loved one dies. Statistics show that grief does not discriminate; it happens to everyone regardless of your age, race, gender, social class, or religious preference. Grief normally presents itself in stages: 1) shock and denial, 2) pain and guilt, 3) anger and bargaining, 4) depression, reflection, and loneliness, 5) the upward turn, 6) reconstruction and working through, and 7) acceptance and hope (www.recover-fromgrief. com).

Grief is a process, and it will change you as you go through it. A considerable percentage of people who've attended to a dying relative, spouse, or friend over a period of time will tell you that one of the feelings they felt when that person died was a sense of relief (griefrecoverymethod.com). As much as I missed my dad and wanted him to be here with me, I was relieved that he no longer had to endure the pain and frustration of being confined to a bed and unable to live a life of independence.

My Transformation

I began this journey broken, sad, conflicted, and unsure of how I was going to go on. I never experienced loss or grief in such an Earth-shattering way, and I didn't know if I could recover from it. My best friend, my batman, my biggest supporter, my dad was no longer here with me, and I needed to find the strength to go on. Although I am still dealing with his death and missing him, I have my own life and the rest of my family that needs me. My heart will forever love and adore my dad; however, these are the things I do to help me be productive while I deal with the pain of grief.

7 Steps to Handling Grief

1. Accept the fact that this is happening. – Many times, we are not able to start the healing process because we will not allow our minds and hearts to accept the fact that this is really happening. It is imperative that you are present in these moments and that you accept the fact that this is happening to you, but you can and will get through this.

2. Feel through it. – This was the best advice that my best friend gave me right after my father passed. In the times that I wanted to shut down and block out my feelings, it was when I allowed myself to feel the pain, cry, scream, be angry, and be an active participant in my grief that I became stronger and able to really understand how I felt.

3. Find an outlet. – Find an outlet like journaling, exercising, crafting, painting, etc. Channel your energy into something productive. You need to find something you enjoy that will help you focus on positive things when you are feeling down and depressed.

4. Build a support system. Join a support group. – You cannot do this alone. I don't care how strong you are. You need someone to talk to, and you need someone who will listen to you without judgment. Grief counselors are educated and can provide you with tools to help you as you grieve the loss of your loved one. They know what the different stages of grief look like, and they can meet you where you are in the process.

5. Lean on GOD. – You need to have someone bigger and stronger than you to make it through the pain of losing your loved one. It is in those times that you need an ever-present friend. You can always call on GOD. When you can't find the words to say, HE can understand your tears, your sighs, and your moans. Let GOD in and lean on HIS Word for strength and guidance as you face this unfamiliar territory.

6. Take one day at a time. – Rebuilding your life after losing a loved one is a marathon, not a race. It will take time to understand, process, and heal from your grief. People know that you are hurting and that you will go through ups and downs throughout the grieving process. You don't have to rush things. You simply need to face what has happened and get through it one day at a time.

7. Be gentle with yourself. – You have survived a traumatic loss, so be gentle with yourself. Give yourself all the time you need to heal and rebuild after this significant change in your life. Every day will not be a good day, but you will get through this. You will realize that you are stronger than you ever thought you could be.

Every Day will Get Better

You will make it out of this journey better than you were when you went in. I promise you that you will look back on this period of your life and say with pride that "I survived what I thought would take me out!" If you hold on, keep praying, and keep moving forward, every day will get better! I know because I went from pain and suffocating sadness to healing and rebuilding after the loss of my father.

XOXO CeCe

CHAPTER 5

FROM DRUG ADDICT
TO FREEDOM ADVOCATE

D. Arlando Fortune

From Drug Addict to Freedom Advocate

Have you ever felt like you were useless? Like people didn't want to give you a chance just because you'd made some mistakes in the past?

I know that feeling all too well. My father told me I had to be twice as good as the white kids because I was black. So, I focused on being at the top of everything I did. But I never wanted to stand out too much for fear of being singled out and pushed out of the club. The club everyone liked. And it nearly cost me my freedom.

My name is D. Arlando Fortune. I am a daddy, authorpreneur, speaker, and self-publishing strategist. I help small business owners and speakers write and monetize books to grow their businesses and share their unique messages.

I share that to give you the understanding that what I'm going to say may not be exactly for you. Being an entrepreneur and a speaker requires confidence, aka personal development, like no other profession. You must see your truth, believe your truth, and share your truth.

As you read my story of transformation, I'll share my truth with you. I ask you to remove the goggles you've been wearing. The goggles you've been viewing the world through have painted it in one light. To be successful in moving forward, you'll have to expand your perspective and grow.

What you're going to read is how I went from physical, mental, spiritual, and emotional imprisonment by feeding my drug addiction to taking control of my destiny and becoming an advocate for freedom using books and entrepreneurship. With that thought in mind, do me a favor and adapt this mantra:

"I make life happen every day!"

My Story

I didn't look like the "typical addict" because I had the appearance of success. Let me make it plain. I had a good life. There's no doubt about that.

So, why on God's green Earth would I destroy my life?

Honestly, I didn't think I would. I was cocky like that. I figured I could stop doing drugs any time I wanted. I'd proved it several times. The funny thing about proving you're not an addict is that people who are not addicts don't try to prove to people they're not addicts.

My story is not unique. There are millions of addicts who are living lies. But God did not place you on Earth to enslave yourself to anyone or anything.

My stints in and out of jail and abandoned houses and hanging with drug dealers has taught me a lot. Most of it is ugly. My story starts in a different area of town. Let me take you back to the beginning.

I was an Army brat. My father moved our family around a lot when I was young. I spent some of my elementary years in Mississippi, Texas, Germany, Iowa, and Illinois before moving to Indianapolis. My father got out of active duty to improve my chances of getting an athletic scholarship.

Maybe the nickname my mother gave me will illustrate my point better. One day, we were looking at our team photos. Of course, I'm looking for myself in the picture. My mother was, too. Then, she starts laughing. Through her laughter, she says, "You're a dot." Confused, I looked down at the picture again, thinking she'd seen something I hadn't. Before telling you what was in the picture, let me give you more context.

In high school, I was a varsity letterman in two sports, part of the accelerated learning curriculum (which meant I took collegiate-level classes) and worked in the dean's office as a peer facilitator. In the evening, I was someone else. I smoked. I drank a little. I tried to fool around with any female pretty enough to catch my eye. I was full of myself. Everyone knew I was on a path to becoming someone great.

So, it was a shock when I was suspended from playing baseball during my senior year. I'd been one of the team captains since my sophomore year. But I got caught up when I decided to skip my last class to get high, eat McDonald's, and mess with girls. The class I was skipping was called Senior Science Seminar. When the engineering firm I was working at called the principal's office to check on me, I got kicked out of the program. That meant I didn't have enough credits to qualify for athletics. I played the second half of the season, but it hurt my averages.

Luckily, the traveling baseball team I played on put me in front of scouts from all over the country. The day I hit the game-winning home run is the day I earned a full scholarship to Howard University. A few weeks later, the Notre Dame coach offered my father a full scholarship to play on his team.

I was later told the Notre Dame coach wanted to know who I was because my name wasn't on his list of players. That's why my mom was laughing at the picture. I was the only black kid on the team. I was the dot on the photo.

When I later learned that I was not given the same opportunity as the other players, even though I was in the top 3 of every offensive stat, it hurt. No matter what I did to excel, I was still sidestepped. There was nothing I could do if I played by everyone else's rules.

Good thing Howard University was an HBCU (Historically Black College University). I would no longer be subject to the flightiness and whims of white America, at least not for the next several years.

The College & Adulthood

I entered college with a white girlfriend and promptly displayed her picture on my desk. As you'd expect, that relationship didn't last. To say I took it hard would be an understatement. I was devastated. I took to drinking heavily, smoking weed, and moping around the campus. That semester triggered a spiral of addiction that would later put me in a concrete box facing 12 years of prison.

The beginning of my decline wasn't that bad. I got over that woman. It took years of self-medicating and self-therapy. One day, I decided I was through with being afraid. I was going to be so wealthy that no woman would dare leave me.

These are my results. After graduating from college, my second year working for the government went like this:

Totaled my Mountaineer after passing out at the wheel.

Arrested for soliciting an undercover cop.

Sentenced for possession of paraphernalia and two seeds and stem of marijuana.

Put on a deferment program for drunken driving.

I was making a lot of bad decisions. My family made my next one. I was to go back to Indianapolis to live with my parents. The decision seemed to be working, too. For the first couple of years, I completed my probation, held down a job, and started buying rental properties.

I thought I had things figured out. I had a vision board in my basement with all my goals on it. I was in culinary school, learning how to be a chef. I had rental income and a mentor to show me the real estate game.

Then, I had an idea.

What if I took the thousands of dollars in rental money I had in my pocket and flashed it around at my favorite watering hole? (Okay. So, I was young and liked to frequent strip clubs with my friends at the time.) With all that money in my pocket and a new level of cockiness, I proceeded to "blow" my money on drugs and partying.

That's when things began spiraling out of control. I selfishly put my needs in front of my family, my tenants, and God. After that, I did a lot of things I'm not proud of, but there is a silver lining.

However, it got a lot worse before it got better (as it is with most negativity). This is what happened. I was on a mission "boosting" liquor from local stores when I got a phone a call. It was a woman I'd been trying to hook up with for a while. Tonight was my night. I took a quick calculation of the inventory rolling around on the backseat. From my estimation, I'd have enough for a hotel room and a quick meal if I hit one last store.

That one last store is what cost me a fun night, my freedom, and ended my brief stint as a street hustler for druggies and drug dealers. I made it out of the store with the goods and got arrested after fighting the cops in the parking lot.

My Transformation

Sitting on a bunk in jail the next day, I realized the gravity of my situation. The three-strikes rule stated I would receive full punishment for my crimes – 12 years of imprisonment.

I wanted to change, and I didn't want to go to prison.

Your mindset determines what you do with the dominion God gave you at birth. These are the steps – as I see them – that led to retaking control.

While in prison, I promised God I'd be different if He showed me how and gave me a chance. I didn't understand Him when my journey began. All I knew is that I had to work on myself physically, mentally, spiritually, and emotionally.

I exercised daily. You'd be surprised how many routines you can create to stay fit when you're focused.

I asked my sister for books because I have a firm belief that you're only one book away from your next breakthrough. I highlighted those books - and others I borrowed from the library - with colored pencils.

All of this work, and I couldn't do much about my emotions. I meditated and prayed. I didn't need to show my cards or emotions to those predators. I had to act or not act. Those were my options. Emotion was a weakness to be exploited. So, when I was released, I had wounds that had not been tended to.

It was a twelve-step program and drug court that helped me change. Drug court kept giving me chances to get my act together; the twelve steps helped complete my spiritual connection by dealing with the emotional wounds from my past.

God can't steer a parked car. Once you start moving towards a goal you believe He's called you to do, then He will send you the guidance you need.

Overcoming

To achieve your mission, you'll need three things: attitude, beliefs, and commitments. Your attitude determines how you move forward. Will you succumb to your challenges or make them submit to your persistence? Will you be a servant leader or step on the people around you? I had a decision to make when I sat in jail, and when released, I chose a growth mindset.

Your beliefs are critical because you won't do something you don't believe you can do. You don't need 100 percent belief. You need enough to try. You can borrow the belief from God, family, friends, or others until you build up your self-belief. I was blessed to have a family that still believed in me. I also had the members of the twelve-step program who believed I could change my life.

The final piece is commitment. We do the things we're committed to doing. Fear shows up, and your unwavering commitment defeats it. Failure shows up, and you accept it because you recognize it's part of the process. Discipline grows out of your steadfast commitment. It is the antidote to average results.

The ultimate transformation is a result of aligning your attitudes, beliefs, and commitments towards your personal mission with the support of your Higher Power. You've just learned what that looks like in my life. You've also received the steps to doing it for yourself. My secrets, shame, and sadness kept me sick. They kept me away from the blessings God had prepared for me.

I'm grateful for my successes and failures. I'm grateful for being locked up. I appreciate being able to say I'm a grateful, recovering addict. For when you become grateful for it all, you realize you don't ever have to return to the person you used to be.

You're reading these words because your spirit led you here. You asked for a solution. That was you deciding on your personal mission. If you are to succeed, you must keep moving forward following "Good Orderly Direction." Remember your mantra. Say it proudly. Do it proudly. "Make LIFE happen every day!"

CHAPTER 6

GETTING LAID OFF PAID OFF

Dr. Adrienne Michelle Horn

Once you graduate from pharmacy school,
what exactly do you plan on doing with your life?

The answer was most certainly not entrepreneurship. I wanted to be a pharmacist. Nothing more, nothing less. After pledging a few organizations, working a full-time job, and studying for an average of five classes at a time, I was ready to jump into my career and discover the answer to that question one day at a time. Shifting from the classroom to my career was difficult, but being laid off, losing my six-figure salary, and becoming a business owner was even harder. School didn't prepare me for this, but I quickly expanded my thinking and transformed my worries into something beyond wonderful.

I was always fascinated by the power a pharmacist held. My mother, my uncle, and my aunt worked in the same field. I quickly learned I didn't have to stand behind a counter and speak to countless patients as I worked a 12-hour shift if I didn't want to. And I didn't want to. So, I made up my mind that I wasn't going to. I wouldn't fall into a career simply because someone told me it sounded like a good idea, or I would make a six-figure salary. I wanted something that would set me up to be "well off" and "successful." I was determined to wake up every morning and smile, knowing I chose a profession I absolutely loved and live a life I, at one time, could only dream of.

After being unable to obtain an internship or residency of any kind due to my having to take care of my mother, who had been diagnosed with breast cancer, I finally landed my first job in Miami Beach, FL, most commonly referred to as South Beach. One year after I had graduated with my doctorate, I was presented with this amazing opportunity to work for an up-and-coming compounding pharmacy that would soon be transitioning into the mail-order realm. I would be creating policies and procedures that would help the company do its part in improving patient care on a national scale. I was thrilled! I had done it. I had been offered a position as a working professional I was not qualified for and would be working in a place many people would kill for.

Life was starting to look up for me. I was well on my way to comfort, stability, and career advancement. I was 25 years old and reaching milestones that our society believes serve as indicators that a person was headed in the right direction and would eventually "make it." According to Forbes, less than 50% of U.S. workers feel that they have a good job. I had a great job and could thankfully say I was a part of the number of employees who were actually enjoying their careers.

During the Christmas season of 2016, I was very much happy with my position. In a little over a year, I had jumped from a five-figure salary to a six-figure salary, become the regional director for the corporate office, and managed to become a licensed pharmacist in FOURTEEN states all while raising my one-year-old-daughter, Paris. Given the plight of our workforce during that time, I was beyond thankful to still be employed. Many companies had lost their best employees simply because they could no longer afford to keep them, and here I was still receiving raises and bonuses.

When I entered the building the week before Christmas, I walked into my office and stared out of the window, looking toward the beach as I did every morning. The view was nothing short of breathtaking. When I looked down at the sidewalk, I saw so many walking in their designer outfits without a care in the world. I smiled because, in many ways, I felt like I was one of them. I was living my best life at a young age, and to me, that was a beautiful thing.

I walked to the Keurig and made a fresh cup of coffee as I ran through a list of things I needed to get done that week if I had any hope of having a great Christmas with Paris. Being that I had missed her first birthday by 15 minutes (the flight was delayed) due to work, she was owed at least that. I picked up my pile of mail from the tray at the front desk and planned to go through all of it as soon as I checked my emails.

It was 8:00 a.m., and I already had issues requiring my attention. *This a problem that needs to be resolved BEFORE Christmas. We can't go into the new year this way. I will make sure to schedule a meeting AFTER the holiday season. They won't be focused, anyway. Ugh! Another denial? Why can't the licensing coordinator ever get these applications correct?*

As I attempted to juggle the plans for work in my mind, I was halted by an email from the Chief Executive Officer of the company. It read:

Dear Dr. Horn,

Today is a sad and difficult day for all of us, but the time has come where we must address the present so that we can prepare for the future. While your dedication and work ethic has been exemplary, we will be closing our doors this year. Effective January 7, 2017, we will no longer need you to report to work.

Sincerest Regards,

S. C.

I must have read that email ten times before the tears started to fall. I was in complete disbelief. I had everything I could have ever wanted, and with three sentences, it was all taken away from me. I went above and beyond the call of duty every day with little to no complaints. I missed my daughter's birthday for a work emergency for Christ's sake. And what did I get in return? A pink slip. I had officially been laid-off.

I was scared for my life. I had just moved into a brand-new townhouse and had a helpless one-year-old to take care of and a Christmas to plan. I had no one to turn to, but God, and He just didn't seem to be moving fast enough. My racing heart had plummeted to the pit of my stomach and made me nauseous for what seemed like hours.

There was no Plan B. All I knew how to do was maneuver around office politics, secure my promotions, and help make the company profitable. In an instant, I was mentally unhealthy. My stress level was through the roof, and I forced myself into a state of anxiety by constantly questioning whether or not depriving myself of sleep and working on the weekends had been enough. Was I enough?

In January 2017, the U.S. Bureau of Labor Statistics reported that 1,659,000 individuals had been laid off of their jobs, and I was one of them. The laughing and playing that was reserved for my daughter on the weekends had been replaced with creating cover letters and revamping my résumé. By society's standards, I had come to a crossroads and selected the wrong path.

For as long as I can remember, I had this overwhelming desire to meet the approval of others. I pushed myself to be a straight-A student in high school, a leader in my community while in college, and an outstanding professional within my career. But that fire was gone, now. I wasn't happy anymore because I had become the one thing I vowed never to be – a statistic. However, it didn't take me long to realize I had a choice to make. I could either continue doing what I was doing, or I could branch out and try something new.

I had been laid-off for about two months and could not secure an interview with anyone. Sunday through Saturday, I spent more hours than I can count situated at a table with Paris in my lap looking for my next place of employment. The opportunities that were posted on various job boards seemed great, but I apparently was not a great fit for those positions. I felt the pressure of paying bills and taking care of my family as the funds I had dwindled to nothing.

I was desperate and figured that maybe it would just be best to go back to school to obtain my master's in public health. I always said that I would eventually go back to school, and I knew I was competing with hundreds, if not thousands, of others who had earned the same degree I had. However, I quickly removed that thought from my mind when it dawned on me that it would not be the immediate solution for a very emergent problem I had yet to resolve.

I will never forget the morning when I received an inbox message from a Facebook friend asking if I still did freelance editing. I had minored in English in college and edited essays and term papers to make additional money before I started working at a call center full-time. With the state I was in, there was no logical reason to tell him no. We needed the funds badly. I quoted him a price and proceeded to edit the poems he wanted to include in a poetry book he had planned to release that summer.

I finished the project that day, and he was extremely pleased with my work. To this day, I don't know what made me ask him if he knew anyone else that needed my services, but I did. The one trait that I have always possessed is ambition. I had come to a point in my life where I realized I had to channel that ambition into something creative if I was going to survive. After talking to my best friend that afternoon, I decided I would be an editor if I could not be a pharmacist.

I wish I could tell you that transitioning from being a pharmacist to becoming an entrepreneur was a seamless process, but it did not work out that way. I had to work small projects to get the funds I needed to hire the help I needed to help me make the money I needed to take care of me and my daughter. I continued to search for a job in the pharmacy industry, hoping that my résumé would be appealing to someone, but it did not happen that way. Life had pushed me off the diving board. I would either sink or swim. I chose to swim.

During my transformation, I was the most successful because I allowed myself to:

Be Bold – I had the courage to leave what was familiar and go after something that was so unlike anything I had ever done. Because of my decision, I have inspired others to follow me on my journey as an entrepreneur.

Be Teachable – I immediately surrounded myself with a community of individuals who had become entrepreneurs themselves. Listening to them allowed me to make fewer mistakes than I would have had I tried to do it on my own.

Be Consistent – I promoted myself and my services every single day without fail, even when I didn't feel like it. Your credentials do not equate to your potential. If you dedicate yourself to accomplishing your goals, you will triumph over every obstacle.

Be Creative – Don't be afraid to explore all of the gifts that you have been given. Each of us possesses something that can be beneficial to others. Once you discover how to convert your gifts into gains, the possibilities will be endless.

Be Faithful – Prepare yourself for the odd looks and awkward conversations with your friends and family. At the first sign of trouble, many will try to discourage you and tell you that it is a terrible idea. However, pray and stay the course. Great things always await those who are patient.

When I was laid off from my job, I lost my paycheck, my health insurance, and my 401K. It was sudden and completely unexpected. It would have been so much easier if I had been allowed to continue my desired path to career advancement. It was comfortable and familiar. However, if I had not experienced such a terrible time in my life, I may not have ever discovered all that I was capable of.

Being jobless gave me the push I needed to start my own editing company. Although it was initially a solution to a problem I knew I needed to solve quickly, I grew and learned so much as I built a new dream from scratch and watched it manifest in my reality. The process was not easy. I encountered a lot of opposition from some I thought would encourage me the most. However, once I took responsibility for myself, I went from being an insecure and jobless mother to a successful six-figure entrepreneur and speaker. You, too, are more than capable of achieving this same level of success, so don't you dare let anyone else tell you differently.

CHAPTER 7

DR. DISABILITY

Dr. Janell Jones

The Façade

Have you ever acted like you had it all together, but deep down, you felt like you weren't enough?

That was my story. If you looked at me from the outside, you'd think I had it all together. You'd see a strong and educated Black woman, one who is a powerhouse and a go-getter. You'd also think I was fed from a silver spoon. Why? Because that was the appearance I worked so hard to create. I didn't want to hide from where I came from, but I hid from what I still struggled with. I hindered myself and the opportunity to liberate those around me. Even though I knew where I came from, I hid the full me from the world.

Telling my story is not new. I've had formidable experiences such as early childhood trauma, teenage pregnancy, and divorce. However, this will be my first time telling one untold story - I suspect that I have a learning disability. I haven't been officially diagnosed with dyslexia, but as a licensed clinical therapist and being familiar with the DSM-5, my symptoms align with the diagnosis.

I am telling my story to those who also have any type of learning disability and feel they are unable to achieve their dream, unworthy, and inadequate and need to have certain accolades to be successful. The truth is, I was able to gain massive success despite my learning challenges. It started with an inside job. I had to accept myself and thrive in my flaws. I was able to obtain an associate's degree, a bachelor's degree, a master's degree, and an honorary doctoral degree. I went from feeling unintelligent and having low self-esteem because of my learning challenges to getting a doctoral degree and teaching women how to how to heal and authentically walk in their purpose.

Not So Uncommon

There are several types of learning disabilities; dyslexia, dyscalculia, dysgraphia, to name a few. Merriam-Webster defines a learning disability as "a condition that interferes with one's ability to learn and results in impaired functioning in language, reading, writing, math, and reasoning and is believed to be caused by difficulties in processing and integrating." While many children are diagnosed with learning disabilities that carry into adulthood, there is an alarming number of adults who have an undiagnosed learning disability. I felt it was important to highlight all learning disabilities, not just dyslexia. It's imperative to understand that success can be achieved despite the challenge.

As mentioned, I believe I have dyslexia. Mayo Clinic states that dyslexia is a learning condition that includes trouble reading due to problems identifying speech sounds and learning how they relate to letters and words. Simply put, it is when individuals have issues decoding.

It has been estimated that 1 in 6 adults struggle with reading difficulty. With dyslexia, Austin Learning Solutions reports that 40 million adults in America have dyslexia, but only two percent are aware. Additionally, 20% of school-age children have dyslexia, and 50% of NASA employees have dyslexia. The number increases for African Americans and Latinos and those in public schools (The Yale Center for Dyslexia and Creativity).

Many in the African American and Latino communities fear receiving inadequate treatment due to the stigma and repercussions associated with a learning disability. Those who continue to go undiagnosed run the risk of low-self-esteem, underemployment, and mental health issues. In the US, studies indicate that the number of minorities with learning disabilities is largely due to social inequities. Adults with undiagnosed learning disabilities have suffered silently, and many will continue to go undiagnosed due to a lack of resources and awareness. Nevertheless, bringing awareness and providing diagnostic tools can change one's life by giving them the help they need to overcome the learning disability.

Girl Interrupted

Remember that silver spoon? It was just the opposite. I grew up in poverty in the projects of Columbus, Ohio. I was the youngest of six children, of which five of us had different fathers. My mother was an alcoholic- suppressing her own issues- who grew up during segregation. Even though I grew up in the projects where drugs overtook the neighborhood, I felt the love in the community. Looking back, most of my family members probably had a learning disability, which can be hereditary. Education was not a priority, and you struck gold if you didn't become a teenage parent and graduated from high school. I was only one out of two; I became pregnant at 16 and had my first son at 17.

I had an interest in college after high school and enrolled in two community colleges, but I didn't feel like I would succeed. Therefore, I did not pursue higher education. College and trouble reading and writing, please! It wasn't until I was almost 30 years old with a high school diploma, working at a job that I tapped out of that I decided to take a leap of faith and go to college.

My Why

I began my studies at the University of Phoenix, which was challenging because it was an online school that required more discipline. I knew that if I didn't do something with my life, I was going to remain in the same position. The struggle was definitely real because it took a great deal of time to read through the material and comprehend it. I did all I could to understand and retain the information, and I used memory to my advantage. I dreaded writing papers and put it off to the last minute. The thought of writing increased my anxiety.

In middle school, I used to hate being called on to read out loud. I was placed in a reading intervention course based on the previous year's standardized testing. In the seventh grade, while we were reading *Sarah, Plain, and Tall*, I mispronounced simple words. My classmate burst out laughing, and the other students joined in. My classmate mocked me almost every day for about a week.

Fast-forward to my early forties, and I was required to read out loud during a job training. My gut wrenched, sweat filled my palms, and anxiety pounded my chest. I skimmed through the slides before it was my turn to read, just to be sure I knew how to pronounce the words. This happened often. I was afraid that people would question my intelligence because I struggled with reading.

No one knew I struggled with reading. The few people who did know wondered how I was an author with reading and writing difficulties. When I was around people who I perceived as being smarter than me, I shrunk and dimmed my light. If they said something I didn't understand, I would nod and move on to the next topic. This stole my confidence for many years and aided in low self-esteem.

I had trouble retaining the information that I read. The words and letters scattered the paper. I had a hard time focusing and would lose track quickly. My mother wasn't an advocate for education since she dropped out of high school in the ninth grade and was born in an era where survival was more important than education. Therefore, I often felt alone until my children started experiencing the same issues in school. My daughter, like me, learned to hide it, but my son was often in trouble.

I felt that I wasn't good enough because I struggled with reading. Honestly, it held me back many years because I thought I couldn't do what I loved -- tell my story. I wondered who would listen to me or take me seriously. I was afraid to go to college because I thought I would fail. This affected my self-love, self-esteem, self-confidence, and my outlook on life. Where would I get with only a high school diploma? I had already spent years on welfare. Those big dreams of being a teacher seemed farfetched.

My why became important to me. Although I struggled with reading and writing, I knew that I couldn't quit. My why was my three children because I wanted them to see and do more. My why was my mother. I wanted her to be proud of me. My why was my family. No one had graduated from high school. My why was my future self. I knew that God created me for a bigger purpose.

Beyond The Limits

The Ohio State University was much more intimidating for me with a learning disability. Not only was it one of the largest universities in the United States, but you had to physically attend class. That meant my hidden secret would now be exposed. But my why became bigger than my fears. I went on to graduate from The Ohio State University with a bachelor's degree in social work with honors (Manga Cum Laude) and a master's degree in social work. I also became an entrepreneur, best-selling author, international speaker, certified life coach, and a therapist.

Here are my seven transformational steps that helped me get through.

1. **Understand your learning difficulties/disabilities.** People cannot change what they don't know or seek to understand. This is defined as misuse. Understanding your learning difficulty will allow you to give yourself grace.

2. **Seek help.** Don't be afraid to seek professional help and support from friends and family. There are stigmas attached to seeking help that's entrenched in embarrassment and shame. Seeking help is perceived as a weakness and, therefore, prohibits others from getting the help that's imperative to their growth. Many people have researched, gone to school, and practiced how to help you cope with learning difficulties.

3. **Disconnect learning disability from being unintelligent.** I often felt I didn't belong in rooms because people were "smarter" than me. Having a learning difficulty means that you process things differently from others. There are many brilliant, successful people with learning disabilities.

4. **Advocate for yourself.** You have to fight for your rights (because you have them). Having a learning difficulty doesn't assume mistreatment. You have to stand up for yourself.

5. **Learn your learning style.** It is important to know how you process information since you receive information differently. This can mean it takes a little extra time to read. I am a kinesthetic learner, where I learn by doing. If someone explains something to me, it goes over my head. However, if you physically teach me, it sticks.

6. **Know that you're not alone.** Millions of people suffer from learning difficulties and have similar struggles. When you isolate yourself and feel no one understands what you are going through, you will not thrive, and the stigma of having a learning disability will debilitate you. Find ways to connect with people who face

71

similar challenges. You can join support groups, both in-person and online.

7. **Thrive in your strengths.** It is very easy to focus on your weaknesses, the negative. Instead, excel at what you're good at. I was very passionate about being an author and helping others, but the grammatical errors, organization, and lack of comprehension caused anxiety and dread. What I learned to do was outsource the grammatical corrections. Otherwise, I wouldn't be an author

Free At Last

I'm liberated in telling my story of having a learning disability because I realize it doesn't define me, and I can help others reach their dreams. I am glad I didn't give up on myself because now I have the confidence I need to reach my wildest dreams. If you get anything from my story, get this: there is nothing you cannot do if you truly set your mind to achieve. Many people with a learning disability have had monumental success, such as Jim Carey, Justin Timberlake, Whoopi Goldberg, Tom Cruise, Daymond John, Malcolm-Jamal Warner, Steve Jobs, and Albert Einstein. Owning your disabilities means owning your life.

Resources

http://dyslexia.yale.edu/
https://www.merriam-webster.com/
https://austinlearningsolutions.com/blog/38-dyslexia-facts-and-statistics

CHAPTER 8

SUCCESS AND HEALTH

Kisha L. Clarke

*"For I will restore health unto thee, and I will heal thee of thy wounds,'
saith the LORD" ~Jeremiah 30:17*

Living with an illness is both a challenge and a blessing. I have conquered renal failure, feeling like a failure, and I am now living a favor filled life. It has framed me into the woman that I am today, manifesting both my strengths and weaknesses. I will share with you my personal tale of secrets, sadness, and shame that I have experienced in dealing with illness, dialysis, and kidney transplantation and how I healed from it.

Understanding Kidney transplantation & Dialysis

Kidney transplantation: a surgical procedure to place a healthy kidney from a living or deceased donor into a person whose kidneys no longer function properly. (Renal failure)

Dialysis: a lifesaving treatment to artificially simulate kidney function. Blood is filtered either by a machine or in the belly several times a week for several hours at a time.

According to The National Kidney Foundation, over 100,000 people are awaiting a kidney. The median wait time is 3.6 years, and on average, 3,000 new patients are added to the registry each month.

Kidney transplantation is not without risk, as with any surgical procedure, but is one worth taking as it has changed the quality of my life exponentially.

"Celebrate endings - for they precede new beginnings."

~ Jonathan Lockwood Huie

My Journey

"You have Lupus. But you're not going to die."

I was thirteen when I heard those first words in the doctor's office with my father at age thirteen. Years later, on a Friday, that same conversation would occur; only this time, it was a different doctor, and I was twenty-seven.

"You need a kidney transplant immediately, and you will have to begin dialysis on Monday."

I felt the oxygen leave my body. *Transplant? Dialysis?? MONDAY??? I need more time!* I looked over at my father and felt such sadness. My mother had died of Lupus when I was two years old. Was he inwardly panicking and thinking that I would meet her same fate? I was devastated. I knew about dialysis and did NOT want to do it. It was at that moment that I decided that I would not be on it for long as my faith was the strongest part of me.

The doctor asked if I had any questions, and I gave her a resigned "no." How could she answer the burning questions in my head? *Who will want to marry me now? What man is going to find me attractive with battle scars and tubes from dialysis and surgery? Not to mention the side effects from the medicine... Yeah, that's appealing.*

As time passed, I decided to keep the temporary catheter in my chest against the advisement of the doctors and nurses since the surgical procedure to connect a vein to an artery for dialysis did not work. *Ha! I told you I wouldn't do this for long*, I thought. The insertion of the temporary catheter did not go without challenge either. Because I was so thin, my lung was collapsed in the process. The pain was unreal. I just sobbed in my hospital room.

It was a lonely and long process, sitting connected to a dialysis machine. Four hours is a long time to think three times a week. I thought a lot about my life and how I felt cheated. My dreams were not just deferred but snatched away. Although I presented as happy, confident, and assured, on the inside, I was inherently sad. I felt like a fraud. I'd masked my side effects and aches with accessories and smiles. I felt like a burden to my father. *I* was supposed to be taking care of *him*. I blamed myself for his fret and concern.

I felt like a failure in my career. Although I had a budding radio career in another state, I lost it due to illness. I was in renal failure at that point and chose to return home to begin dialysis. I was terrified that if I began a career in Television Broadcast Journalism for which I was trained, I would not be able to hide my health situation. My puffy cheeks, occasional limped gait, and achy joints would be a dead giveaway that I was unable to honor the charge of my contract. In addition to that, I would be talked about by the audience in unkind ways. In my fragile state, I knew I was not ready for that. I was scared and deeply saddened that I would live a life of unfulfilled dreams. I was in a secret and solitary state of depression.

"A crown, if it hurts us, is not worth wearing." ~ Pearl Bailey

The partners whom I'd chosen were emotionally unkind. I had allowed myself to be disrespected and unappreciated as I did not demand that I be treated in a manner that every woman should want to be treated. If I could not see the diamond in my reflection, how could I expect others to see a gem?

I remained in unkind relationships much longer than I should have. When I was told that I would not be wanted by anyone else, it validated my own self-narrative. I replayed all the conversations which I held with myself and subsequently agreed.

As the months progressed, I began to feel more and more defeated. I was seeing the side effects of the medication and losing self-confidence. My cheeks were puffy, and I had tubes sticking out of my chest. I was achy and tired all the time. I was sometimes dizzy the day after dialysis. I fainted one morning and had to be rushed to the hospital as too much water was removed the night before on the machine.

"Depth of friendship does not depend on length of acquaintance"

~ Rabindranath Tagore

I was convinced one evening to attend a party with some friends. I really did not want to go as I was not feeling up to it. I went anyway and met a man who, in a few months, became my dear friend. We would talk for hours about everything, including my health; something that I did not readily discuss with many people. I always felt that if I shared my health issues with someone, they would think lessor of me or show pity. He did neither. He treated me like a true friend, and I love him for it.

My new friend was concerned about my health and informed me that he was donating his kidney to me. I said, "Sure. Thanks," and continued with our conversation. He repeated it on three more occasions and was met with the same answer. I'd heard this before from many well-intended people. It was not until he had bloodwork and psychological testing done that I believed him. He was a perfect donor match, sharing my uncommon blood type held by less than 10% of the population in the US. He volunteered that God directed him to do it, so he listened.

On December 18, 1998, a little over a year after beginning dialysis, my friend and I went into surgery. I do not remember if we saw each other before it, but we woke up together in the ICU. Groggy, he asked why I was yelling.

Apparently, the anesthesia had worn off sooner than anticipated, and I'd awakened confused. I think I was just over it all and was ready to leave and start my new life—just a theory.

We stayed approximately a week in the hospital with our rooms close to one another. We had many family members and friends who visited and prayed for us. I quickly learned that laughter was literally painful. That, of course, did not matter to them nor me.

After receiving my lifesaving kidney, I wanted to be a mom more than anything. I was married, and God had answered my prayers with a baby. This inspired me to work on myself. I knew that I had to be whole, especially for my son. I knew that my job was to give him the best of me. Four different doctors told me that I should *not* even consider it, as it would have put my life in jeopardy, but I trusted God.

"I love the person that I've become because I fought to become her"

~ Kaci Diane

My marriage was another unhealthy relationship, but I was hopeful that it would improve. I believed in love and wanted a family. Unfortunately, it ended after lasting fourteen years. I knew that this would be the final relationship in which I was unhappy and felt devalued.

It took me years to rebuild my confidence to the point where I KNEW in my spirit that I was worthy of a viable and blissful relationship. I was blessed with a son and felt that he deserved to have the mother for which God intended. How could I raise a confident person if it was absent from myself? I prayed tirelessly and knew what my next step had to be.

The day that I left my unhealthy marriage was both devastating and galvanizing congruently. It was the genesis to my new confident life. I was terrified but no longer felt less than smart, beautiful, or competent. I felt a renewed sense of confidence and peace. Leaving was an extremely difficult decision, but I felt it was the right one.

Studies have shown that a person's thoughts, feelings, and beliefs have a crucial effect on their biological functioning. After the conclusion of my marriage, I began working on *me* with various motivational and spiritual practices. By doing so, it encouraged emotional healing, and my body followed in kind. Not only was I happier, but I felt stronger. I've compiled a list of steps that were implemented which were pertinent to my healing:

1. **Prayer.** I am in constant conversation with God. It's a good thing He never tires of me.

2. **Meditation.** I focused on the things for which I was grateful. It made me look at all of the beautiful things about myself; inside and out. I had a renewed appreciation for my blessings; my son, health, family, friends, career, and relationship with God. It also helped me with the forgiveness of my former husband and myself.

3. **Exercise.** Walking, cycling, swimming, and lifting weights. Yoga is also a great way to still the noise and focus on the body.

4. **Spending time with family and friends.** I've hit the jackpot with them.

5. **Laughter.** See #4

6. **Introspection.** I evoke the many challenges that I have conquered to remind myself that I am one strong cookie.

7. **Painting.** It is very relaxing and allows my creative side to flourish. In my mind's eye, I am ready for my first exhibit!

8. **Writing.** I often journal, and it is extremely cathartic. It allows me to process all of my feelings and experiences. It helps me to audit my growth and put everything into perspective. It is a good practice with which to complete the day along with prayer. Hmmm, maybe I'll write a book...

9. **Traveling.** It was difficult to do during dialysis and something that I promised myself I would continue after my transplant. I have kept my promise.

10. **Reading.** I love biographies, and it was my way to not only glimpse into the lives of others but also a way to become inspired by their journeys.

11. **Continuing a career that was put on hold.** Also adding another career as an Author.

12. **Being Mom to my favorite person in the entire world.** The best part of my healing.

13. **Music.** I love various genres of music. Listening to and recreating music on a keyboard also makes me happy. This was one of the things my son and I did together when he was a toddler, and it brings back great memories.

Life Today

I have now been living with my kidney for twenty-two years. I am a pescatarian, exercise daily, and recognize my value. Living with an illness is a journey of hills and valleys. Of course, there are days where I may not feel or look my best, but it is no longer because I feel unworthy. I love myself and continue to have an amazing relationship with God.

My donor is my son's Godfather and is doing well with a family of his own. In addition to writing, I have begun a successful career as a Voice Over artist, which I love. God has many ways in store for me to inspire others, and I am excited to see what He places before me next.

I have the most amazing, bright, witty, talented, kind, supportive, and loving son who amazes me daily. He is the best part of me, and I thank God for him **and** am proud that I give him the best of me.

*For more information on kidney transplantation,
contact the National Kidney Foundation at kidney.org

CHAPTER 9

HEALTHY LOVE AFTER ABUSE

Larsche Reaves

When I decided that I wanted more, then I was no longer willing to settle for less. I endured years of pain and uncertainty, yet I maintained my smile. However, I am breaking my silence and voicing my experience from physical abuse to prove that there is a way out of an unhealthy relationship. I no longer fear the unpredictable behavior knowing that I deserved better. I want others to know that they, too, deserve to be loved in a way that does not hurt physically. The purpose of my story is to encourage young adults to evaluate their relationships to ensure it is best for them. Now, I'm not saying the road is easy, as it is rough, but there is happiness on the other side of abuse. Come with me on this journey so that I can show you how I went from being confused and bitter as a result of physical abuse to becoming humble, loving, and the recipient of real love.

Physical abuse is the non-accidental force that results in injury, pain, or impairment. It is also used by the abuser to control the victim. Physical abuse can happen to both men and women. In the United States, there are 20-24 people per minute being abused by their intimate partner. This equals to more than 10 million abuses annually, with about 5 million women as young as 18 and 3 million men. This statistic is alarming. As much as we are embarrassed to talk about it, we are not alone.

It Was Simple

I was raised in a two-parent household and stayed around my family and friends a lot. I was the only child at home, and I didn't lack anything. Although I didn't need anything, I started working at the age of 14 just because I felt that I wanted money of my own. However, this didn't last too long because I could not get time off work when I wanted it.

After quitting, I didn't get my next job until my senior year in high school, and that was only because it was a requirement for class. I had a normal life for someone my age.

I stayed out of trouble as I didn't like drama or arguing. I definitely didn't like listening to my parents argue. I stayed to myself as I figured that's just what old married couples did from time to time. I didn't see any real struggle between my parents. In my eyes, everyone was enjoying life with no worries. I was on the dance team at school, and this helped me stay in shape and keep my head clear. I often went to the mall and the movies with my friends and sleepovers with my family.

I became close to a guy in my junior year of high school, and he was really sweet and fun to hang around. I slowly began drifting a little from my family because I wanted to be around him. When we became a couple, I was so happy! We joked and laughed all the time. I couldn't imagine him doing anything wrong or hurtful.

It was senior year and time for senior prom. I wanted to go so badly, but he didn't want to go for various reasons. Being that I considered his feelings over mine, I didn't go and hid the disappointment. Due to my desire to please him, there were several senior events that I missed out on. I even became distant to some friends.

The Change

After graduation, our relationship reached a different level. He was changing and getting angry over the smallest things, but I figured he just had bad days; we all have them. One day at the gas station, he got in the car and was quiet. Before I could process what was happening, we had gotten into an argument that resulted in him slapping me. He had accused me of looking at another man walking by, which was completely untrue.

He soon apologized, saying that he didn't know what had come over him. I figured that he realized that he hurt me, and we would work through it. Things seemed to be ok for a while afterward. There was no real arguing until one night after he hung out with some friends. He claimed that he was told that I was getting close to someone that I didn't even know, and when I defended myself, I was punched in the nose and called names that I had never been called before.

Unsure of what to do and unclear on what had just taken place, I left immediately and had a friend accompany me to the hospital to check if my nose was broken. I definitely hid this from my family. As time went on, after several apologies, I stayed with him but was very skeptical.

Later, I became pregnant and thought that it would change for the better. Oh, how I was wrong! There was a time where I was 1.5 hours late for my OB appointment because we had gotten into yet another argument. He accused me of putting the baby before him. While I was driving, he became ridiculously upset and hit me in the face. He said that I was not attractive, and no one else would find me attractive either if he ever decided to leave. He began hitting me in the face often.

We broke up momentarily, but it wasn't a time of healing and moving forward; it was very stressful. I was dealing with hormones and the stress of this relationship that I was trying to leave. It was hard because he continued to try and sweet talk me, but when it didn't work, he would flip and call me all the names that you could think of. By this time, I had friends but not the same circle as before because I put him before everybody. As time was drawing near for the baby's arrival, he acted as if he had changed and felt bad for everything that he had done to me. Yes, you guessed right. I forgave him.

Enough

After giving birth, his temperament and attitude seemed to change in a good way. We couldn't go back to how we were, but it seemed as if we were starting new. This was ongoing for a couple of months, so I let my guard down a bit. I honestly felt that things were better. However, he had a moment of relapse, which led to a lot of arguing over simple things.

The day that changed me was an argument that led to me being choked in front of my baby, who was propped up on the sofa. I couldn't live this life or allow my child to think that this was right. I did fight back, and soon enough, he realized that the baby was there. I left with my child and told myself that I was done completely and would handle everything that came moving forward.

The rose-colored shades that were over my eyes were finally peeled, and my reality had set in. I made sure to distance myself as I was no longer living for myself. I started to become bolder because now I was protecting my child.

Unfortunately, my leaving resulted in me being stalked. He showed up at my door and said that he just wanted to see the baby. With my guard up, I let him in. He spent a few minutes with the baby before turning to me and asking, "So, are you really going to leave me? You don't love me anymore?"

I replied, "Love doesn't hurt physically, and if so, it isn't for me."

He tried to hug me, and I pushed him away. He got really angry, started calling me out of my name, and said that no one would want to be with an ugly woman with a baby. I told him to get out, or I would call the police. That did not help the situation.

He grabbed me, and I tried to get out of his grasp by pushing him. However, before I could run away from him, he slapped me, and I fell down a flight of stairs and hit my head on the wall. All this happened while my child was in his crib.

I was in complete disbelief. He was not even man enough to see if I was dead or alive. After he ran out of the house, I called the police and was so thankful that they came quickly. I was sitting in the house alone with blood all over my face as I held my six-month-old in my arms. I couldn't tell the police where he went. I later discovered he had been dropped off to my house.

The police wanted to call an ambulance to take me to the hospital because they couldn't tell where the blood was actually coming from. The female officer helped me clean my face to see the true injury. I chose to drive myself to the hospital, which ended in me getting stitches. I was advised to get a restraining order, which I did do.

Secrets, Sadness, and Shame

I didn't want anyone to know what I was going through, so I masked as much as I could until I had to get stitches. Being that I chose my partner over people that really cared about me and who tried to advise me that things weren't going to get better, I was completely embarrassed. This caused me to be more distant and isolated from friends and family. I no longer loved myself, and I felt so stupid because I saw the path but ignored it. Although I was experiencing extreme sadness, I had to hold it together for my child. My heart ached for my child because he deserved better than to grow up with a monster as a father. This affected me for a very long time.

I became very bitter. I learned how to stand up to him, but the verbal abuse and the stalking continued for a few years after. He thought that I was just "upset," but I was angry, fed up, and refused to accept the "temperamental love."

Overcoming Abuse

As I said in the beginning, this road was rough, but I had to do it. In order to better myself, I had to:

Leave: I removed myself from physical abuse by leaving the relationship.

Prayer and Support: I needed an outlet to voice my feelings. I prayed, talked to a friend, and journaled about my feelings to help me to find peace within myself.

Forgiveness: I forgave myself for going back and staying as long as I did. I had to forgive myself for making this choice for my child but understood that my child is who saved me. Ultimately, I forgave him also.

Redirect: I was very angry and bitter for quite some time after the official break up. I eventually had to ask myself what was the benefit of being angry and bitter. Without an answer, I decided to redirect the frustration to work harder to let it go so that I could be happy.

Acceptance: I had to learn to accept that this was a part of my life that I survived! There are so many who did not make it out alive, but I did. I also had to accept that I was a single mother and understand that it was ok.

Self-love: I didn't think that I could ever get to this place. I began to love myself through prayer and positive affirmations.

I am free now and living a better life. I'm glad that I found a way to deal with my inner insecurities resulting from the physical abuse, and I let go of being angry and bitter. By letting go, I have become humble, loving, and I found unconditional love that does not hurt.

If you are overcoming this type of relationship or at the point in which you realize that you deserve better, know that the point of happiness is around the corner. Know that you will love yourself again. Real love will find you, and you will experience greater things as long as you don't give up on yourself.

CHAPTER 10

PRETTY FOR A DARK GIRL

Sharita Davis

You are so pretty for a dark girl.

Who would think that a compliment could be an insult? After all, they are saying that you are pretty. However, it is the subliminal message that a dark girl cannot possibly be pretty that causes the issue. It's almost as if somehow, you are the exception. This is a backhanded insult at its best!

It is time to talk about why we have tolerated such an insult for so long. Women are more likely than men to suffer from poor self-image. Women of dark skin tones have an increased likelihood to have esteem issues. Therefore, they need to be uplifted and encouraged. Our images of beauty often exclude darker skin tones. It is difficult for a young woman of a dark complexion to find a reflection of beauty similar to hers. During a critical time when a young woman seeks to identify her true self, low self-esteem can creep in.

There are subtle subliminal messages sent to our youth. We say, "Black is beautiful," but only present beauty in an undiversified way. I want to see a generation of women of all skin tones living healthy and balanced lives being represented well. I especially want to see strong black women of dark skin tones with healthy views of themselves in society. It's personal because I have a beautiful brown skin daughter and beautiful brown skin granddaughters.

Colorism

Colorism is a term that was first used by Alice Walker in 1982. It was given a name at that time, but the influence has existed in America since slavery. Colorism is a form of racial discrimination based on shades of skin tones.

It causes serious mental and emotional problems that can be passed down generations. It's a toxic legacy.

Skin tone affects the quality of life. Studies have shown that it defines success and affects your ability to find work, and even your ability to find a spouse. Colorism tends to affect more black women than black men. Black women tend to have more negative mental attitudes against themselves. Beauty standards suggest that light is beautiful and dark is unattractive. It is embedded in our social norms, and only 25% of the world's population has dark skin. I have to dispel the myths that skin tone denotes character, mental capability, and beauty.

Colorism is rarely discussed. However, it affects most households. It is difficult to obtain a specific statistic, but it causes serious mental and emotional effects that can be passed down for generations. Studies show that light-skinned black people have higher incomes, complete more years of education, and live in better neighborhoods, all due to discrimination based on skin tone.

Black men have a subconscious preference to desire women with lighter complexions. It is important to discuss this topic to dispel the mentality that skin tone denotes character, ability, and beauty. By dispelling this myth, the mental state, and the quality of life of black people will improve. Colorism has been an ugly bruise starting from slavery, but can be healed by exposure, conversation, and reversal of mindset.

Colorism is a form of racial discrimination based on shades of skin tone. It crosses ethnic barriers but also lies within ethnic groups. I plan to expose the challenges of colorism within the African American community.

I was born to a mother who had a light skin tone and father who had a dark skin tone. Your mother is your first role model, and your first images of beauty are learned from her. However, I did not see myself in my mother because her image was so distant from what I saw in my reflection.

Despite my mother's attempts to build self-worth and esteem, I still could not connect pretty with me. I could not see pretty when I saw my reflection. My skin was too dark to be considered pretty. No one resembling my complexion was considered beautiful.

As I grew into a teenager, my esteem did not improve. I could not identify with models because most models did not look like me. Those that did resemble me were considered exotic. However, I didn't want exotic. I wanted normal, and I wanted pretty.

Relationship Therapy

I experienced multiple failed relationships during my teen years. My first experience at love was at age fourteen. I was introduced to him by a mutual friend. Our first encounters were by telephone only. I prolonged our meeting. If I could get him to like me before he saw me, maybe he would stay with me? My view of self was low. If I didn't like what I saw in the mirror, then why would he like it?

That relationship led to me becoming a teenage mother. My longing to be loved and to be desired led to me seeking love in the wrong way. That pregnancy caused me to feel like I disappointed my mother. I felt as though I brought shame to my family. This led to many years of tormenting thoughts and struggles with esteem. I felt like a failure. I had failed my mother, God, and myself.

Those feelings were further fortified when the relationship did not last. Those feelings of self-resentment intensified. I loved my daughter, but I felt I failed her by not maintaining a relationship with her father. Despite my self-defeating thoughts, I graduated from high school with honors. I felt I needed to excel in academics because I had to make my mother proud again.

My mother taught me from an early age to have faith in God. We attended church services multiple days a week. My faith in God was her gift that saved my life. The teachings I received from a young child began to combat my life of negative thinking.

In my college years, I began to see myself differently. My circle of friends increased. I was introduced to a variety of different people. My view of beauty began to change. Beauty was now diversified. I joined a sisterhood of beautiful, articulate, bold, and successful women. I can now find pretty girls that look like me. I can identify pretty with me. My dark skin tone was no longer a shame.

I suffered years of shame. I walked with my head down. I always sat in the back when there was a crowd. I was shy. I was soft-spoken or silent. Public speaking brought fear and shame. No one around me had any idea that I suffered from low self-esteem.

I suffered in silence. I was ashamed of how I felt about myself. However, I did not know how to change it. That is why my poor self-worth was such a secret. People assumed I had it all together. I still couldn't enjoy the reflection in the mirror. I was completely confused when I was called pretty. Although I hated being called pretty for a dark girl, I never said anything. I remained in silence.

That silence remained until I finally found my voice. I found my voice in the house of God. It was my love of God that finally caused a shift in my thinking. I began to form my own relationship with God. For most of my life, I attended church because of my mother. One day, I decided to go for me. I began to take notes and read my Bible daily.

I went from a quiet and insecure child due to colorism to a bold and confident leader in my church and profession. It was not an overnight transition. There were steps taken to promote this transition.

Step 1. *Change Your Mind.* Transformation has to begin with a change of mind. My change of mind began when I chose to see myself as God saw me. I used scriptures from the Bible to create a change in my mindset. As my faith in God grew, my confidence grew. Knowing that God saw me as greater helped to increase my self-confidence and self-love.

Step 2. *Positive affirmations.* I used scriptures from the Bible as daily affirmations to combat the negative views and feelings of low self-worth. Each day I would force myself to stand in the mirror and look into my own eyes and speak life into myself through the Word of God. Though it was extremely uncomfortable in the beginning, there came a time when I began to believe the words that I spoke. I no longer believed the lies that I had internalized. As my mind changed, my vision began to change.

Step 3: *Open up.* I had to choose to allow people to assist in my personal development and growth. As my self-confidence grew, I began to surround myself with those who looked and thought as I now believed. No longer did I see myself as unattractive, less intelligent, and unworthy to be heard. I now had the confidence and boldness to assert myself and be heard.

I found that I actually had something to say. I was no longer shy and reserved; I was able to speak openly and boldly. Certain people became midwives to this new emerging person. Several individuals pushed me into my destiny by providing opportunities and forcing me into public speaking roles despite my fear and reservation.

Step 4: *Talk out loud!* As my confidence grew, my love of self grew. No longer was I hesitant to look in the mirror. I no longer cringed at the view that society said didn't exemplify beauty. I began to see that person looking back at me as pretty and maybe even beautiful at times. My inward transformation was now showing outwardly. I could associate beauty with a woman of a dark complexion. I no longer felt the need to alter anything that I possessed to conform with society's version of beautiful. I finally realized that I was beautiful because I am fearfully and wonderfully made.

Step 5: *Give Back.* It is now time to pass along what I have learned and unlearned. I have a generation of young women coming behind me being taught not to love themselves if they look a certain way. More specifically, I have a daughter and grandchildren who look like me. I need them to be confident, bold, and self-loving. If they never ingest the ill effects of colorism, then they won't have to reverse them later. Self-love has to start early. Your skin complexion should not affect your life in any way.

This transformation is on-going. My cellphone alarms every day at 6 a.m. to prompt me to repeat my daily affirmations. If I catch myself walking and looking down, I have to correct my posture and look forward. I force myself to look in the mirror without makeup and tell myself that I am beautiful.

I am freer because I no longer ascribe to those negative thoughts as a lifestyle anymore. I am not less because I have dark skin. Nothing can have the power to hold me in a box. God has a plan and purpose for my life. It is my goal and desire to complete them. When those negative thoughts come, dispel them. Do not let them linger. They will make a home.

I am glad I didn't give up. I now see the fruit of my labor. My daughter and my granddaughters walk in confidence. I love it when I see it. If I had created a wound of low self-worth based on skin tone and appearance, my legacy would be destroyed. My children would not be able to see their worth.

My advice to all females, but especially those of darker skin tones, would be to look in the mirror and love what you see. You are not exotic. You are not the exception. You are not abnormal. You are the apple of God's eye. You are not pretty for a dark girl. You are pretty.

CHAPTER 11

CHURCH HURT

Pastor Cassandra Brown

Church Hurt

"Church Hurt" is what is defined as a pain that is inflicted by religious institutions. It separates the person from the church community and from God. The church, which I loved so much, ended up hurting me the most. I'm breaking the silence about the church hurt that I've experienced. I will also share the voices of individuals whose stories differed but experienced the same hurt.

In The Beginning

As a little girl, I could remember being so excited to go to church. Not just on Sundays but just in general. There was something special about the older ladies in the church sneaking me a peppermint and telling me not to tell the other children. I couldn't wait to tell them because it always made me feel special. From singing in the choir to the church dinners to the preaching of the Word of God, it all made me fall in love with the church and the people of God. What I experienced later in the church would rock my world.

Research

I did some research and solicited the church hurt experience from four different people. The first person that I interviewed battled an addiction, which was known by everyone in the church. This particular person shared that they were criticized by congregants each time they went to the altar. The church should be a place where we can come and ask for prayer without feeling judged. This person felt that they couldn't trust anyone to talk to, especially not ask for prayer.

The second person that I interviewed experienced a life of being raped and molested. They felt that instead of the church embracing them with love, reminding them that God was there and that they were in a safe place, they heard whispers as they walked by. This person was never invited to any functions outside of the church, even though invites were being passed around for different social events. They felt like the biggest mistake they made was sharing their story about what they experienced as a child and adult. They felt judged, and their credibility was questioned. Needless to say, this person was already dealing with trust issues. This experience made them not want to attend another church ever again.

The third person felt that church folks were "two-faced." They felt that while in church, they would fellowship and praise God together happily, but as soon as they would see some members outside of church, they wouldn't speak. This bothered them to the point where they felt they weren't good enough!

The fourth and final person that I interviewed battled with sexual identity. They couldn't find where they "fit in." Even though they struggled with who they were as a person, they never struggled with loving God. They weren't looking for anyone to agree nor disagree with what they were going through; they just wanted to feel accepted and be given the opportunity to worship. They felt unwelcomed and never had the feeling that they would ever be accepted in a church. They then decided to never step foot in another church!

Speaking with these people made me see that people are affected by church hurt in many ways. It can either strengthen you as a Christian or weaken your faith walk with God. The church building holds God's people who should not experience church hurt by its members. They should not only feel the love of God but feel God's love in each person.

My Church Hurt Experience

My mother gave me the best gift ever, and that was taking me to church. As I became older, I had an adult body and was being introduced to the street life.

At the age of eighteen, I thought I was grown, and no one could tell me anything! I did a lot of things that weren't Christ-like. I had an attitude that if you came for me, I was coming for you. I was *that* girl at the party. I made sure that you remembered me. I smoked, drank, and loved to cut a rug on the dance floor. One thing for certain was that I loved God and could feel a tug in my spirit that God wanted to use me. I remember being in a club one night, and I turned down every drink that people wanted to buy for me.

I was sitting at the bar when suddenly I heard a Christian song being played in the club! I was sitting there tripping and walked over to the DJ booth and asked him why he was playing that song. He looked at me and said he didn't even know himself what just happened! I grabbed my jacket and left.

As I was driving home, I started to cry out to God because I knew that He was telling me that he wanted my full attention, and it was time for me to surrender.

I was excited to go back to my first love, and that was church, but it wasn't as easy as I thought. What I realized was that the church folks remembered what I did in the streets, my poor choices, and believed gossip that they heard about me. They formed an opinion of dislike, and, most of all, believed that I had no place in ministry. What they didn't know was that inside, I was the same little girl who sat on the church pews clapping her hands and praising God. They didn't know the little girl who would take part in foot washing at the church. The church wasn't there when God called me to preach the Gospel! God didn't need the approval from them, and neither did I. I kept asking God whom in the church would listen to me because I'm not perfect and was a hot mess. The church folks already had a fit about my short blonde hair, ruby red lipstick, and of course, how I could wear high heels while praising God! The church had already marked and judged me. I remember wearing a long dress, blazer, and a bare face with clear lip gloss to church one once. Guess what? They still had something to say about me. It didn't matter what I wore. I felt I would be judged regardless. This was when God spoke to me and asked if I was going to accept the calling of the ministry or if I was going to keep running from Him because I had been hurt by the church. I knew that it was time to surrender and stop focusing on the church hurt and look at what Jesus did for us all on the cross. I knew that it was time to pick up my cross and carry it.

Transformation

When I got into a quiet place with God, He showed me His master plan, and I was finally ready to receive it!

I went from a woman who was hurt by the church and whose faith was at a low to becoming a Pastor. Not only am I a disciple for Christ, but most of all, a woman of God who loves people. I wanted to share my experience of church hurt because I got through it, and you can get through church hurt and any other kind of hurt. Here are the keys to overcome after being hurt:

Overcoming from Church Hurt

1. Prayer: My first step was to pray! Prayer is what got me through. I knew that through this process, I had to keep talking to God because I didn't understand why we hurt each other, especially if we call ourselves Christians. Praying renewed my strength in so many ways. Jeremiah 28:12 (NIV) says that you will call on me and pray to me, and I will hear you. This scripture was confirmation to me that God heard my cry! All I had to do was call on the name of the Lord and just talk to Him. Prayer is a direct communication to

Christ. The more I prayed, the more I was ready to heal and move past church hurt. I no longer wanted to be a victim, but I was ready to become victorious and walk in my calling from the Lord.

2. Decisions: You get to choose how you respond to church hurt or any other kind of hurt. You decide to either stay in a place of hurt or heal. Church hurt can have you in a place where everything in you can be affected, from your worship to your relationship with Christ. Psalm 40:2 (NIV) says that "He lifted me out of a slimy pit, out of the mud and mire, He set my feet on a rock and gave me a firm place to stand." I knew that God pulled me out of that pit, and I could feel Him carry me to a solid foundation and tell me, "Stand daughter. The time is now!"

3. FORGIVENESS! Once I decided to heal, God showed me I had to forgive! Forgiveness had to happen so that I could move on. I could no longer carry the hurt or the grudges towards the people who I experienced the church hurt from. Was it an easy process? NO, but it was needed. God told me that I may not ever get the apology that I deserved, and I had to be ok with that. While learning how to forgive the people who hurt me, God would show me the reasons why I needed to love them. That's what I love about God. I wanted Him to make me better. Isaiah 53:5(NIV) shows me the love that Christ had for us. "But he was pierced for our transgressions. He was crushed for our iniquities; the punishment that brought us peace and by his wounds, we are healed." Christ did all of that for us, so who was I to hold a grudge? Yes, I was hurt, and yes, you may have been hurt, but look at what God did for us! He gave His son up to death so we could live. Now that's love and forgiveness all in one. Jesus did that for us on the cross, and that was enough for me to forgive with or without an apology. This process wasn't easy for me, but I was needed because I was ready to heal and move on.

4. Transformation of a new mindset! Romans 12:2 (NIV) says, "Do not conform to the pattern of this world but be transformed by the renewing of your mind." Then you will be able to test and approve what God's will is; his good, pleasing, and perfect will. Once your mind is transformed, you begin to think clearer. A transformed mind in the body of Christ will triumph over hurt and pain. Once my mind was changed in a positive way, I found myself praying for the people who hurt me. I had fewer tears of hurt with more tears of joy. Most of all, I did not want to keep talking about church hurt in a negative way. When the conversation was brought up about church hurt, I found the good in church and even in the people who may have hurt me. Even when I was struggling with moving forward, I would always ask myself, "What would Jesus do?" I knew Jesus would do the right thing, so every day, I strive to do the right thing. (1 John 1:9) says, "If we confess our sins, he is faithful and just to forgive us our sins, and to **cleanse** us **from all unrighteousness**." If your mind isn't changed, you will remain in that slimy, muddy pit.

5. DON'T GIVE UP! There will never be a perfect church, but there is a perfect God. Being hurt by the church made me feel some type of way about Christ, and that wasn't good. I began to doubt Him in my faith walk. I finally realized that I not only quit church, but I also quit God! I gave up on both. I loved going to church to worship, and once that stopped, I no longer wanted either one. Hebrews 10:25 says that "not giving up meeting together as some are in the habit of doing but encouraging one another, and all the more you see the day approaching." I knew that I needed to be in a house of praise. I knew that my presence was needed not only to worship but encourage someone who may feel like I did, and the people I interviewed did. A hug, a smile, or even saying hello and welcome can make a person feel welcomed in the church. How could I do this if I sat at home feeling sorry for myself? I was excited to go back to the place that hurt me to love on the people of God! I was ready to serve!

6. It's time to walk it out! Matthew 20:14 (NIV) says, "Many are called few are chosen." After going through the steps to heal, I was ready to walk in my calling, and I pray you will be ready as well. I needed to share my testimony and tell the people who were hurt how I made it over. The enemy wants us to keep our mouths shut so people can stay in a place of hurt, in a pit, but most of all, their faith walk with God can be destroyed! This mess of church hurt is now your message to help someone else heal.

7. Repeat the process! The bad news is that church hurt happens more than once. It will come in different forms, but it does come again. But the good news is that the same God that healed you before will heal you again! Philippians 4:13 says that "I can do all things through Christ that strengthens me." Not some things but All things. I ate this scripture daily. As God strengthened me, he showed me my purpose, my calling, and my anointing. It was up to me to let go so that I could heal. Are you ready to heal?

SALVATION

It's time for your new journey to begin! God is ready to do a new thing within you. God has prepared your journey not only to heal but to help others who have experienced church hurt. I not only minister in the church, but I also minister on the street to people who may be overlooked based upon appearance. This is your season to spring forward, and it starts by you accepting Jesus as your Lord and Savior.

"That if thou shalt confess with thy mouth the Lord Jesus, and shalt believe in thine heart that God hath raised him from the dead, thou shalt be saved."

(Romans 9:10)

ABOUT THE AUTHORS

Ayanna Mills Gallow, M.B.A

Ayanna Mills Gallow, M.B.A, is an international bestselling author of books that were self-published by her company, Thanx-A-Mills, LLC—a company where she uses her voice and published writings to inspire, strengthen, and help others overcome adversity. Through her company, she also teaches writers to become authors and authors to become bestselling authors. She enjoys coaching authors to create multiple streams of income from their books.

Ayanna was raised in Freeport, NY, and she currently lives in Alpharetta, GA with her two sons, Colby and Caleb, who are both bestselling authors at the ages of 9 and 12. Ayanna's purpose is to be an intersection between the Bible (God) and the community (Hip Hop) to create success. Her goal is to help others Heal Internal Pain (HIP) so that they can have Happiness, Opportunities, and Prosperity (HOP). She was recently honored with a Community Award for impacting lives with her writing from Women of Integrity, Inc., and she has been asked to join *Innervision Magazine* as a creative contributor and as vice president of operations.

Ayanna is also an advocate for African American boys and men to help strengthen families and relationships in the African American community. In 2019, Ayanna was ordained and licensed as an Evangelist. Ayanna went from being silent due to childhood trauma to becoming an author and public speaker focusing on topics of overcoming, success, purpose, women in business, and the glory of God.

Ayanna can be found on Instagram and Facebook at ThanxAMills and at www.thanxamills.com.

Amika Reynolds, M.D.

Amika was born in Jamaica, West Indies as an only child to Sandra Mitchell and Ronald Reynolds. At a very young age, she migrated to the United States, where she resided in the Bronx, New York. Amika's education has brought her from New York City to Philadelphia to Antigua and, ultimately, to Kingston New York, where she completed her residency in Family Medicine. Amika is board certified in Family Medicine and currently practices medicine as a Nocturnist in Nyack, New York.

Amika is also a mother of two young girls who she adores.

Amika hopes that one day her skills in medicine will expand across the globe to help others who need excellent healthcare.

Brian Lewis

Brian Lewis is a chef, Outdoorsman, and first-time author/project manager of this book "Free from Silence." As an advocate for children, Brian has dedicated time as a youth football coach and mentor to kids in his community. Single with no kids of his own, Brian credits his 40-plus nieces and nephews and days at the Boys & Girls Club for his dedication to the well-being of children.

In the past five years, Brian has worked as a sous chef and kitchen manager for some of the most beautiful National Parks in America. (Yellowstone, Denali, Death Valley) Brian currently lives in Girdwood, Alaska, researching for his next books. Brian will be releasing his children's picture book "The Adventures of Brian the Bear" December 2020 while finishing his novel "Kodiak" whose set date has yet to be determined.

Chanel Rose-Budd

Chanel Rose-Budd, A Relationship, and Personal Development Expert, Ordained Minister, Author, and Philanthropist

Born in Pittsburgh, PA, and now a 17-year resident of Dallas, TX. Chanel's personal journey of working full time, being a young mother, and then becoming a wife led her to be inspired in assisting others in accomplishing their goals and dreams and building and renewing relationships and skillsets despite the barriers by overcoming them during the process.

Life, as we all know, has its challenges, although we all have a choice to allow them to stop our growth and success or not. I challenge all who connect and work with me to beat the odds by choosing to grow and succeed in your life individually or as a couple.

"Giving Love & Relationships A Strategic Advantage"

Cylia Williams-Staton

Cylia Williams-Staton began her "now normal" when her father was diagnosed with an incurable disease, and the dynamic of their relationship drastically changed. Their journey created and birthed the story of overcoming grief that she openly shares in this anthology. Her undergraduate career began at Elizabeth City State University and concluded with her earning her BBA from Campbell University. Service to others and dedication to sisterhood led her to become a proud member of The Delta Sigma Theta Sorority, Incorporated (Delta Chi Chapter). Her value of education and love for children drives her daily as a Kindergarten Teacher. She aims to inspire others through her motivational blog "Evolution of CeCe" and always strives to honor GOD and her family. She shares this journey called life with Anthony Staton and her three amazing sons, Camryn, Justice, and Kyrie. Her father, Robert Williams, inspired her to control the narrative of her life and share her story with the world.

D. Arlando Fortune

D Arlando Fortune, or "Fortune" as he prefers to be called, is a former government accountant turned entrepreneur and self-publishing strategist. As an entrepreneur, his main areas of focus are human psychology, drug addiction recovery, and self-publishing. He's the creator of the RACE Formula™, the SIGNATURE Book Formula™, and founder of No Doubt Nation, where the followers live by one mantra: "Make LIFE Happen... EVERYDAY!" With the release of his third book, "The 4-Hour Book", Fortune became a bestselling author and narrowed in on his best service to date – self-publishing strategy. As the mastermind behind the Wealthy Author Podcast and the #OneBookAway Movement, he trains small service businesses and speakers on how to write, self-publish, and convert branded books into multiple streams of income.

Dr. Adrienne Michelle Horn

Adrienne Michelle Horn, a native resident of Miami, Florida, is a young, energetic community leader whose primary focus is perfecting literary projects that will positively impact the lives of those who have an enthusiasm for reading. As a teenager, she developed a love for words and expressed her thoughts through poetry. Although she received her Doctor of Pharmacy and

Pharmaceutical Sciences degree from Florida A&M University, she never lost her passion for reading and revision.

Upon graduating, Adrienne embarked on a journey that would allow her to make a positive impact within the literary world. Fueled by her desire to make her mark as an independent editor in a corporate-driven industry, Adrienne decided to transition her experience by forming her own editing business, I A.M. Editing, Ink. While Adrienne continues to serve the nation in the capacity of a pharmacist, her heart is deeply committed to making the literary world a better place one successfully edited project at a time.

Dr. Janell Jones

Janell Jones is on a mission. Born into poverty and raised in the projects of Columbus, Ohio, Janell lost her father and sister to inner-city violence as a child. A teenage mother at 17, she was nonetheless determined to live a different life than the one she saw played out around her. This fueled her passion to work with youth. That determination also took Janell from an associate's degree in psychology to Honorary Doctoral Degree in Healthcare Leadership. Janell is a licensed social worker in the State of Ohio and practices as a licensed clinical therapist.

She is the founder of Melanin Grace Publishing, LLC, a publishing company- and became a certified life coach and shares the amazing story of how she took the leap that awakened her to her purpose and destiny. Janell created the "Mahogany, Beautiful Bright Me" program to help girls with self-love and self-acceptance. Janell also has the "Girl, You Got This" Podcast.

Kisha L. Clarke

Kisha has successfully navigated life around the challenges of illness and kidney transplant by receiving a kidney that was donated to her by a dear friend. She candidly shares her journey of happiness and pain in this anthology.

Kisha's career began in Gospel radio, and she is now a world-renowned Voice Over Artist whose work can be found in Documentaries, Commercials, Narration, Social Media, Promotional work, Corporate Training, Fundraising videos, and Medical Shows.

She has appeared in a Transplant Health Documentary Series, highlighting patients on dialysis. She has interviewed and directed a segment on The Disabled Person's Channel about Epilepsy.

Kisha is an enthusiast of the Arts, Music, and Literature, with biographies being her favorite go-to literary genre. The Cello is her favorite instrument as her son is an amazing Cellist and composer at age twelve.

Kisha comes from a large extended family whose love and support have been her backbone. She attributes her conquering the many challenges of illness to her family and friends.

Kisha currently resides in Atlanta, Georgia with her wonderful son Joshua and they put God as the head of their family.

Two goals of Kisha's are to develop a mentoring program for young boys and a Domestic Abuse safe house and facility for women and children, which will not only provide shelter but learning and training opportunities.

Her story will show you the strength and fortitude she has to inspire others who may be in the same or similar position and help others dealing with their own health concerns.

Larsche Reaves

Larsche Reaves, born and raised in Atlanta, GA. Owner and Founder of L'sche Logistics, a company that provides Dispatching and Consultation Services for truck drivers. Prior to her current endeavor, she obtained her LPN license and a bachelor's degree in health science from Brenau University. Larsche worked in Healthcare for 11 years in various roles until recently. She was afforded the opportunity to leave healthcare and pursue her journey as an entrepreneur. While following this path, she was given a platform to artistically outline segments of her past. She was able to overcome unfavorable circumstances, which helped form the witty and charismatic women that she is today.

Sharita Davis

Sharita Davis is a registered nurse who has been practicing for 15 years. She is also a licensed minister, worship leader, and entrepreneur. She enjoys sharing her love and knowledge of God, His Word, health, nutrition, and self-care. She has joined her love of God and her professional training to travel and share His Gospel while serving those in need as a missionary. She is also the owner of Raiment by Rita, an upcoming online clothing and scrub boutique. She attended Temple University, earning her B.S. in Biochemistry. During that time, she became a proud member of Alpha Kappa Alpha Sorority, Inc. (Delta Mu Chapter). After working several years as a chemist, her compelling nature to nurture prompted her to pursue a career in nursing. She enrolled in Drexel University's ACE Program, an accelerated nursing program and received her BSN. She is currently pursuing her master's degree in her profession. Her love of God and desire to complete His purpose and plan in her life motivates her to sound the alarm to this generation to be bold for Christ. Her proudest achievements are being a mother to her beautiful three children and two grandchildren. She describes them as her wealth.

Pastor Cassandra Brown

Who is Pastor Cassandra Brown? She's a woman of God who loves souls. She's a Pastor, mother, Glammy (grandmother), and a disciple for Christ. She's a woman that not only serves inside of the church but loves to serve outside of the church. She's a woman that has been through some storms in her life, but God has remained faithful. Pastor Cassandra Brown is that a sinner saved by grace. She's a woman who believes in loving and encouraging the people of God. Maybe everyone will not understand her or her story, but someone will be encouraged and ready to start the healing of church hurt once they finish reading. Remember, she loves you, but God loves you more. Do it, God!

CPSIA information can be obtained
at www.ICGtesting.com
Printed in the USA
LVHW090823010920
664633LV00004B/496